UTHOR

SUSAN MALLERY'S

Fool's Gold Cookbook

Susan Mallery's Fool's Gold Cookbook

ISBN-13: 978-0-373-89281-5

[CIP data available upon request.]

www.Harlequin.com

Printed in U.S.A.

Photography: Michael Alberstat

Fool's Gold Books
by SUSAN MALLERY

Christmas on 4th Street
Three Little Words
Two of a Kind
Just One Kiss
A Fool's Gold Christmas
All Summer Long
Summer Nights
Summer Days
Only His
Only Yours
Only Mine
Finding Perfect
Almost Perfect
Chasing Perfect

Fool's Gold Ebook Novellas

Halfway There
Almost Summer
Only Us
Sister of the Bride

Contents

Introduction

I hosted my first dinner party when I was thirteen. Three friends and I decided it would be great fun. I would prepare a feast and they would join me for dinner and a sleepover. (These days dinner rarely leads to a sleepover, or at least, not the kind of sleepover we had planned, but at thirteen it seemed the ultimate in sophistication.) My mother took me shopping then bravely left me alone in her kitchen to prepare our feast.

In no particular order, here's what I learned from that first traumatic experience: my aunt was wrong. Turning the oven to 350 degrees and baking whatever for thirty minutes does not apply to everything. That when a recipe directs you to apply butter and flour to the baking dish, it's not a suggestion. Orange chicken has nothing to do with cooking chicken in orange juice. And that while preparing a salad the night before because you have a gymnastics meet and won't have time before the party is fine, it's not a good idea to put on the dressing that early. In other words, if you've never cooked before, follow the recipe precisely!

The food was a disaster. There I was—thirty minutes before my guests were due to arrive and I had nothing to eat. Fortunately, Mom came to the rescue and suggested we order in pizzas. We dined in style, had a wonderful evening and a very successful sleepover.

All these years later, I still experiment in the kitchen, but I've taken my cooking disasters to heart and learned from them. I stick with what I do best: plan ahead and keep it simple. This cookbook is filled with easy recipes for delicious food. A couple of recipes might challenge the beginner, but by and large, "quick and easy" is what I gravitate to. Like many women, I'm too busy to spend hours in the kitchen.

I'm not a professional chef. I'm a home cook, just like you. I want to nurture my family and friends with spectacular event-appropriate food, with the least amount of time and effort possible.

I'm also a storyteller. I have always loved telling stories, especially romances. So much so that I've turned it into a career. With more than one hundred romance books under my belt, I think it's safe to say that I'm in this business for the long run.

A few years ago, I started a new series in the fictitious town of Fool's Gold. It's set in the foothills of the Sierra Nevada mountains. Fool's Gold is a friendly place with charming people who bring casseroles to their neighbors whenever there's a life event that calls for it.

One or two weekends a month, the festivals held in Fool's Gold bring street-food tastings to the town. Other days, residents can count on an outstanding meal from one of their terrific local restaurants. When a man behaves badly, the women meet en masse to trash him over decadent desserts and a slushy drink du jour.

The Fool's Gold series started with *Chasing Perfect* and now the books number in the double digits. Readers seem to gravitate toward the recurring characters who make the town feel like home, even sending me their own suggestions for food at their favorite eateries in the town. And thus the idea was born to post on my website, www.susanmallery.com, specific recipes so that readers could enjoy the mouthwatering dishes I described in my books with their own friends, book clubs, family and, of course, love interests.

One day my brilliant editor suggested I consider collecting all the material so we could see what we had. That material became this cookbook.

We've organized the Fool's Gold recipes by season. My cooking philosophy is to make things easy and delicious, using available ingredients. You will find plenty

"a taste of what it's like to throw caution to the wind and fall wildly in love"

of recipes for your family and lots for sharing. But there is something else for you in these pages. A surprise.

As I mentioned before, I am a romance writer. I love the idea of two people falling in love. I adore the sense of community that occurs when two families are drawn together because of a powerful connection. Love heals, love inspires and when combined with delicious food, love is magical.

PHOTO: THIEN LAI/CAPTUS PHOTOGRAPHY

Woven within the pages of this cookbook is a Fool's Gold love story not available anywhere else. It's funny and flirty and my bonus gift to you. For those of you who adore Fool's Gold, welcome back. For those of you who have yet to sample this small California town, I offer you a taste of what it's like to throw caution to the wind and fall wildly in love. Maybe over a Coconut Vanilla Snowball Cupcake.

Regardless of how you came to have this cookbook, please enjoy the delicious recipes. And remember that important lesson from my first cooking experience: it's not the execution of a well-planned meal that matters, but the sharing of delicious food with loved ones. And maybe the promise of an extra-special sleepover. Wink. Wink. My best to you and yours.

Happy cooking and happy reading.

Susan Mallery

CHAPTER 1

Ana Raquel Hopkins knew for sure that Greg Clary was the most annoying man on the planet. He was the kind of annoying that got under your skin and made you want to scream. It was like being in the mood for guacamole, only to discover that someone had taken all your deliciously ripe avocados. Or worse, taken them and made their guacamole out of those avocados and now people were saying it was better than yours. That's how annoying Greg Clary was.

Ana Raquel stared at the sign hanging from the rustic building at the Condor Valley Winery. The hand-carved square of wood said only Café. So simple, so right. While she'd been off studying the art of cooking, Greg had been working his way up the kitchen ranks right here in Fool's Gold. Six months ago he'd opened Café in his uncle's winery and the restaurant was getting rave reviews. Everyone was talking about it. And Greg.

After graduating from culinary school, she, too, had worked in restaurants, but hers had been in San Francisco. After a couple of years, she'd discovered that while she loved making delicious food for people, she didn't love working in a restaurant. A visit to a street fair had introduced her to the magic that was street food—delectable concoctions made in a mobile kitchen. She'd saved her money, bought an old Airstream and had it refurbished as her traveling kitchen. Then she'd brought it home to Fool's Gold, where she planned to take the culinary world by storm.

Only Greg had beaten her to the punch. Again.

Seventeen years ago, when Ana Raquel was in the second grade, she'd been chosen to be Cinderella in the school play. Greg had been picked to play Prince Charming and, in the end, he'd gotten all the applause. In junior high, they'd both run for student council president. Greg had won, leaving her with the runner-up vice-president position. In high school, she'd been nominated for homecoming queen and he'd been nominated for homecoming king.

You can probably guess who won and who didn't.

All of which she could live with, except for what happened the night of their senior prom.

The fancy dinner and dance had been held at the Gold Rush Ski Lodge and Resort, just as it was every year. There had been a band and good food. Most of the teens went in groups, rather than with dates—one of those town traditions, she supposed. For reasons she still couldn't explain, Ana Raquel had chosen that night to confront Greg about all his transgressions.

But instead of going up to him and yelling, she'd found herself mesmerized by his dark eyes and easy smile. And maybe a little by how good he looked in a tux. Still, she'd had righteous indignation on her side and she knew she really should be telling him off. Only what should have been yelling somehow turned into kissing. And kissing turned into, well, you know.

She could have lived with the biggest mistake of her life, except that partway through he'd figured out it was her first time, which meant it wasn't his. Worse, in the middle of the moment, she'd had a second realization. It was the teeny, tiniest bit possible that she had feelings for Greg. Romantic, what-if-I've-secretly-loved-him-my-whole-life kind of feelings.

Talk about a mistake. Greg wasn't just popular, he was a chick magnet. She would have been little more than one more girl who fell for him. Terrified and humiliated, she'd done the only thing that made sense. She'd run off to culinary school in San Francisco.

Now she was back in Fool's Gold and all grown up. She was a nice person, she told herself. Friendly. She liked people and she adored making them happy with her food. If not for Greg, her life would be perfect.

But she had a solution for that problem and an appointment with the town's mayor to discuss her brilliant idea. One that would help her make a name for herself and get over Greg Clary once and for all.

Mayor Marsha Tilson was the longest-serving mayor in California. She was a well-dressed, white-haired woman who loved her town—idiosyncrasies and all. She welcomed Ana Raquel warmly and led her over to her desk.

"We're so happy to have you back in Fool's Gold," Mayor Marsha said with a smile. "You were missed. You're always so friendly and enthusiastic. Even when you were little, you looked out for the other children and now that you're grown, you're feeding all of us."

"Thank you. I'm glad to be here," Ana Raquel told her. "I learned a lot in San Francisco, but it's not the same as being home."

Ana Raquel was one of three girls. Fayrene, her twin, owned a temp agency and pet-sitting service in town, while Dellina, their older sister, ran a party planning and decorating business. The Hopkins women were self-starters.

The mayor picked up a flyer for Ana Raquel's street cart from her desk. "We're getting excellent feedback on what you've been serving. The locals appreciate another place to go for lunch, while the tourists love both the food and the convenience."

"I've been experimenting a lot with different ingredients," Ana Raquel told her. "You know how different food is served at different festivals? Rather than make people wait for their favorites, I'm working on ideas of turning festival specialties into everyday recipes. I created an Elephant Ear Pull-Apart Bread. It suits the season, but gives us a taste of what we miss."

"I've heard your Carrot Cake Muffins are creating quite a stir. There was something close to a riot over them last week."

Ana Raquel laughed. "I ran out of muffins and there were still people in line. It got a little loud there in the park."

The mayor smiled. "I believe that is what they call a high-quality problem. Now tell me about the cookbook you mentioned when you set up our meeting."

Ana Raquel clasped her hands together and leaned forward. "I want to take what I've learned and share it with people on a larger scale. I want to create a cookbook based on the town and what we like to eat here. I thought I could collect recipes from locals who want to share them. I'll also create some of my own. I was thinking the recipes should be delicious but not too complicated. People are busy and not everyone wants to spend all day in the kitchen. We could call it Fool's Gold Cookbook."

She squeezed her fingers, hoping she could hide her sudden nerves. She wanted the mayor to be excited about the cookbook idea.

Mayor Marsha leaned back in her chair. "That's very interesting," she murmured. "I like the concept. Ironically, someone else came to me last week with a similar plan. Given that you both came to me with cookbook ideas, I hope you don't mind that I took the liberty of inviting him to join us."

Even as she spoke, Mayor Marsha was standing and motioning for someone to enter the room. Ana Raquel knew who it was before she bothered to turn around. Because there was only one person who would invade her meeting and steal her idea.

Chapter 2 begins on page 28

sp

Light Meals

Roasted Beet Salad with Farro, Fennel and Goat Cheese

Farro is a chewy grain found at specialty and gourmet food stores. If farro is unavailable, you can substitute barley or brown rice, cooked according to package directions. This salad boasts both color and crunch.

- 3 medium beets, trimmed (or 1 package [500 grams] precooked beets)
- 3 cups water, plus more if needed
- 1 cup farro
- Salt and black pepper
- 1 small bulb fennel, diced
- 1 small shallot, minced
- 2 tablespoons fresh lemon juice
- 1 tablespoon extra-virgin olive oil
- 2 tablespoons fresh tarragon, chopped
- 4 ounces mild goat cheese, cut into small squares or crumbled

TIP: Save time (and red fingers!) by using precooked beets, now available at many markets.

1. Preheat oven to 400°F. Loosely wrap each beet in foil and roast 45 minutes, until fork-tender. Peel and dice beets.
2. Meanwhile, bring 3 cups water to a boil. Add farro and a pinch of salt. Reduce to a simmer; cover and cook 25 minutes, until the farro is just tender. Add water if needed during cooking. Cover pan with a dish towel until ready to use.
3. In a large serving bowl, combine beets, farro, fennel, shallot, lemon juice and oil. Season with salt and pepper to taste.
4. Garnish with tarragon and goat cheese.

Creamy Turkey Salad with Dried Cranberries and Toasted Pecans

Mellow turkey chunks are studded with sweet cranberries and crunchy pecans in this light but filling salad.

- 1 cup mayonnaise (reduced-fat is fine)
- 2 tablespoons fresh lemon juice
- ¼–½ teaspoon Dijon mustard
- Salt and black pepper
- 4 cups cooked turkey meat, cubed
- 1 small stalk celery, chopped
- 1 cup toasted pecans or walnuts, chopped
- 1 cup dried cranberries
- 2 tablespoons red onion, minced, or scallion, sliced
- ¼ cup fresh Italian parsley, chopped
- Romaine lettuce, chopped, for serving

TIP: Round out the meal with a crusty baguette or whole-wheat rolls.

1. In a large serving bowl, whisk mayonnaise, lemon juice, mustard, salt and pepper. Fold in remaining ingredients except lettuce. Line serving plates with chopped lettuce. Top with a mound of turkey salad.

Arugula Pesto, Ricotta and Roasted Tomato Pizza

Sharp arugula stands in for basil in this easy pesto sauce. It's a great way to use up that almost-wilted arugula in your refrigerator.

Serves 4

Pesto

- 2 cloves garlic, smashed
- 1 bag (5 ounces) baby arugula
- ½ cup extra-virgin olive oil
- ¼ cup walnuts
- ½ cup Parmesan cheese
- 1 tablespoon fresh lemon juice
- Salt

Pizza

- Vegetable oil and cornmeal, for prepping pan
- 1 large (1 pound to 1¼ pounds) prepared pizza dough
- 1 cup (6 ounces) ricotta cheese, preferably fresh
- 1 cup grated Parmesan cheese
- 1 large tomato, cored and very thinly sliced

TIP: The sauce recipe makes 1 cup, and you only need ½ cup for the pizza. Use the rest as a pasta sauce, sandwich filling or sauce for grilled meat.

For pesto:

1. In the bowl of a food processor, process garlic until minced. Add arugula, a handful at a time. Pour in oil; process until blended. Add walnuts, cheese, lemon juice and salt; process until smooth. You should have about 1 cup pesto; you'll need about ½ cup for the recipe. Reserve remaining pesto for another use.

For pizza:

1. Preheat oven to 425°F. Lightly oil baking sheet; sprinkle with cornmeal. Roll out dough on a lightly floured countertop to a 10-by-14-inch rectangle. Transfer dough to the prepared baking sheet. Spread ½ cup pesto evenly over dough, top with ricotta, Parmesan and tomatoes. Bake 15 to 17 minutes, until cheese is melted and crust is golden.

Super-Healthy Chicken Salad Wrap

Yet another dinner made easy by using a supermarket rotisserie chicken. Save even more time by using preshredded carrots or coleslaw mixture for the veggies.

- 1 tablespoon fresh lemon juice
- 1 teaspoon white-wine vinegar
- 1 teaspoon minced garlic
- ½ cup plain Greek yogurt (nonfat is fine)
- 1 tablespoon fresh dill, chopped
- Salt and black pepper
- ¾ cup crunchy vegetables (such as carrots, zucchini, cucumber, snap peas), shredded
- 2 large wraps or tortillas
- 1½ cups cooked chicken, shredded

TIP: Omit the garlic if you don't like raw garlic.

1. In a medium bowl, whisk lemon juice, vinegar and garlic until blended. Fold in yogurt and dill. Season to taste with salt and pepper. Fold in shredded vegetables until coated.
2. Lay wraps on counter; divide chicken between wraps. Top with vegetable mixture. Fold up and serve immediately.

Tarragon Tuna Melt

This satisfying sandwich is a go-to meal for a busy weeknight dinner.

- 1 can (5 ounces) solid albacore tuna packed in water, drained
- ½ cup mayonnaise
- 1 tablespoon fresh lemon juice
- 1 small scallion, thinly sliced
- ¼ cup diced red pepper (about ½ small pepper)
- ½ small stalk celery, diced
- 2 tablespoons fresh tarragon or dill, chopped
- Salt
- 1 baguette (about 10 inches long), halved crosswise and lengthwise
- 3 ounces sliced sharp cheddar cheese

TIP: Tuna has such a strong flavor that sharp cheese works best in this sandwich.

1. Preheat broiler. In a medium bowl, combine first 7 ingredients. Season with salt, to taste.
2. Divide tuna mixture on baguette slices and top with cheese slices. Broil until cheese is melted and bubbly.

Greek Salad Sandwich

Don't worry about exact measurements when making this savory vegetarian sandwich—just add ingredients as you like.

- 1 medium tomato, diced
- ½ small cucumber, very thinly sliced (no need to peel)
- ¼ cup green pepper (about ¼ of a pepper), diced
- 1 slice red onion, coarsely chopped
- 2 tablespoons feta cheese, crumbled
- 1 tablespoon fresh mint, chopped
- 2 teaspoons sherry vinegar or red-wine vinegar
- 2 teaspoons extra-virgin olive oil
- Salt and black pepper
- 2 large pita pockets
- 4 tablespoons prepared hummus
- 2 handfuls baby spinach, chopped

TIP: Serve the sandwiches as soon as you make them—otherwise the bread will get soggy.

1. In a medium bowl, combine tomatoes, cucumbers, green peppers, onions, feta and mint. Add vinegar and oil; toss to coat. Season with salt and pepper.
2. Open pita pockets. Spread hummus into each pocket. Stuff pockets with salad mixture and spinach.

Fajita Quesadilla

This recipes serves 2—if you double it, you'll need a large pan to fit all the meat.

Serves 2

6 ounces skirt steak, thinly sliced
1 tablespoon Worcestershire sauce
1 tablespoon fresh lime juice
1 clove garlic, minced
Salt and black pepper
2 tablespoons olive oil, divided
1 small onion, thinly sliced
1 small red pepper, thinly sliced
4 burrito-size flour tortillas
1 cup Monterey Jack or cheddar cheese, shredded

Garnishes

Sour cream
Salsa

TIP: Get 2 skillets going at once and the quesadilla cooking will be done in half the time.

1. In a small bowl, combine steak slices, Worcestershire, lime juice, garlic, salt and pepper. Let marinate 15 minutes.
2. Warm 1 tablespoon oil in a medium nonstick skillet over medium heat. Add onions and peppers, season with salt and cook 10 minutes, until softened and golden, stirring often. Drain liquid from meat; add meat to the skillet and cook 5 minutes, until browned, stirring. Remove to a plate.
3. Warm half of remaining 1 tablespoon oil in the same skillet over medium heat. Add a tortilla; top with half of meat mixture. Sprinkle with half of cheese. Top with tortilla; cook until lightly browned, about 2 minutes. Carefully flip; cook the other side until the cheese is melted and the tortilla is browned. Slide the quesadilla off the skillet; sprinkle with salt and cover with foil to keep warm.
4. Place the skillet back over medium heat; add remaining olive oil. Repeat steps with remaining tortillas. Serve with sour cream and salsa.

California BLT

Ingredient amounts given here are just guidelines—
the exact amounts you'll need depend on the size of the bread slices.

Serves 2

- 4–6 strips bacon
- 2 tablespoons mayonnaise
- 1 tablespoon fresh dill, chopped
- 4 slices challah or brioche bread, toasted
- ½ cup baby spinach or spring-green lettuce leaves
- 1 medium tomato, thinly sliced
- 1 avocado, sliced

TIP: Challah is a soft, rich bread that complements the sandwich. However, any mild bread works well.

1. In a large heavy skillet over medium-low heat, cook bacon until crisp. Transfer to a paper towel–lined plate.
2. In a small bowl, combine mayonnaise and dill; spread on two slices of bread. Layer spinach, tomato, bacon and avocado. Top with remaining bread.

Quick and Easy Nachos

Garnish this family favorite with your choice of toppings—salsa, chopped lettuce, jalapeño, onions, sour cream...

- 5 cups whole tortilla chips (about 6 ounces)
- 1 can (about 15 ounces) black beans, drained and blotted dry
- 2 cups shredded cheddar cheese
- 3 scallions, sliced
- 1 tomato, chopped
- 1 avocado, chopped
- Toppings, as desired

TIP: Keep the chips crispy by microwaving them for the shortest amount of time possible.

1. Spread chips on a large platter; top evenly with beans and cheese. Microwave just until cheese is melted. Top with scallions, tomatoes and avocados. Serve immediately with desired garnishes.

Steak Stir-fry with Snow Peas

Serve this quick stir-fry with rice.

- 3 tablespoons peanut oil or vegetable oil, divided
- 1½ pounds flank steak, cut into thin slices (see TIP)
- ¾ pound snow peas, trimmed
- 4 cloves garlic, minced
- 1 tablespoon peeled and minced fresh ginger
- ⅓ cup hoisin sauce
- ¼ cup reduced-sodium soy sauce
- ¼ teaspoon red pepper flakes, or to taste

Garnishes

- 2 scallions, thinly sliced
- ½ cup roasted unsalted cashews, chopped

TIP: Freezing the raw beef for 15 minutes makes for easy slicing.

1. Warm 1 tablespoon oil in a large non-stick skillet over high heat until very hot. Add half the steak and cook 1 minute, without stirring. Stir-fry 30 seconds, until lightly browned. Transfer to a bowl. Repeat the process with the remaining beef.
2. Warm another 1 tablespoon oil over high heat. Add snow peas and stir-fry 1 minute, until bright green. Push peas to the edges of the pan; add garlic, ginger, and remaining 1 tablespoon oil. Stir-fry 30 seconds. Stir in steak.
3. In a bowl, whisk hoisin and soy sauce with pepper flakes. Stir sauce into the mixture in pan; cook 1 minute. Garnish servings with scallions and cashews.

Coconut Popcorn Shrimp with Mango-Lime Salsa

Don't be daunted by the long ingredients list—
everything comes together in minutes.

Shrimp

- ¾ cup canola oil
- ½ cup all-purpose flour
- 1 cup plain seltzer or club soda
- Salt and black pepper
- ¾ cup panko crumbs or bread crumbs
- ¾ cup shredded coconut (sweetened or unsweetened)
- 1 pound large shrimp, peeled and deveined

Salsa

- 1 ripe mango, peeled and diced
- 1 red pepper, diced
- ½ jalapeño pepper, seeded and diced
- 2 scallions, thinly sliced
- 2 tablespoons extra-virgin olive oil
- 3 tablespoons fresh lime juice
- 2 tablespoons fresh cilantro, chopped
- Salt and black pepper

TIP: Panko crumbs make for a crisper crust. Find them in the Asian food section of your supermarket.

For shrimp:

1. Warm oil in a large, heavy skillet with at least 2-inch-high sides. In a bowl, whisk flour, seltzer, salt and pepper. In a shallow bowl, combine panko and coconut.
2. Dredge shrimp in the flour mixture, then the panko mixture. Transfer to a wire rack to dry slightly. Fry shrimp in the oil in two batches, about 2 minutes per side, until cooked through. Drain on paper towels.

For salsa:

1. While the shrimp cooks, make the salsa. In a medium serving bowl, toss mangoes, red and jalapeño peppers, scallions, oil, lime juice and cilantro. Season with salt and pepper. Serve with shrimp.

Seared Chicken with Lemon Spinach

Dinner in 15 minutes! There's no need to dress the spinach—just drizzle the pan sauce over both chicken and greens. Serve with rice to soak up the savory sauce.

- 1 tablespoon olive oil
- 1¾ pounds thinly sliced, boneless, skinless chicken-breast halves
- Salt and black pepper
- 1 shallot, minced
- 2 cloves garlic, minced
- 1 can (14¾ ounces) reduced-sodium chicken broth
- 2 tablespoons fresh lemon juice
- 2 tablespoons drained capers, rinsed
- 4 handfuls (about 5 ounces) baby spinach leaves

TIP: Tender baby spinach is best for this recipe. Regular large-leaf spinach leaves are just too tough.

1. Warm oil in a large nonstick skillet over medium-high heat. Season chicken with salt and pepper. Cook chicken 5 minutes, until browned on both sides and just cooked through. Transfer to a platter; cover to keep warm.
2. In the same skillet (no need to clean) over medium heat, cook shallots and garlic for 30 seconds, stirring. Add broth; bring to a simmer, scraping up brown bits from the bottom of the pan. Cook 5 minutes, until the broth is reduced to about ¾ cup. Add chicken and any juices from the platter; simmer 1 minute, until heated through. Remove from heat; stir in lemon juice and capers.
3. Place a handful of spinach on each serving plate. Divide chicken among the plates; drizzle with sauce.

Thai Peanut Chicken

Write this recipe down on a card and stick it to your fridge—
it's easy, tasty and endlessly adaptable.

Serves 4

- 1 tablespoon olive oil
- 1 pound chicken tenders or thinly sliced chicken breasts
- 4 cups mixed fresh vegetables (broccoli, snow peas, carrots, bell peppers), chopped
- ½ cup peanuts (preferably unsalted), chopped
- 1 small clove garlic, minced
- ½ cup reduced-sodium soy sauce
- ½ cup reduced-sodium chicken broth
- 2 tablespoons peanut butter
- 2 teaspoons cornstarch
- Pinch of cayenne pepper, if desired
- 2 scallions, thinly sliced
- 4 cups cooked rice

TIP: Want a vegetarian version? Omit the chicken, up the veggies and swap out vegetable broth for the chicken broth.

1. Warm oil in a large nonstick pan over medium-high heat until hot but not smoking. Add chicken; stir-fry 2 minutes, until browned but not cooked through. Add vegetables; stir-fry 3 minutes, until crisp-tender. Reduce heat to medium. Add peanuts and garlic; stir-fry 30 seconds. Stir in soy sauce.
2. Place broth in a small bowl; microwave until just warm. Add peanut butter and cornstarch to warm broth; whisk until blended. Slowly stir warm peanut butter mixture into pan, still over medium heat, stirring to coat vegetables with sauce. Add cayenne pepper, if you're using it. Garnish with scallions and serve over rice.

Easy Sesame Peanut Noodles

Serve this better-than-takeout noodle dish warm or cold.

- 12 ounces thin spaghetti
- ¾ cup peanut butter
- ½ cup bottled Asian sesame dressing
- 2 tablespoons coconut oil
- 1 cup carrots, shredded
- 1 cup cucumber (from about ½ cucumber), finely chopped or shredded
- 2 scallions, thinly sliced
- ½ cup peanuts, chopped
- ½ cup fresh cilantro, chopped

TIP: Commercial peanut butter makes a creamier sauce than natural varieties.

1. Cook pasta according to package directions. Scoop out about ½ cup cooking water just before pasta is cooked through.
2. While pasta cooks, combine peanut butter, sesame dressing and coconut oil in a large serving bowl. Add pasta cooking water to thin the peanut butter and blend the mixture. Drain pasta; rinse in cold water. Add spaghetti to peanut sauce; toss to blend. Refrigerate 1 hour until cool, if desired. Toss with remaining ingredients before serving.

Fettuccine with Citrus-Parsley Pesto

Pesto sauce takes on an unexpected flavor twist with the addition of orange juice.

Serves 4–6

- 12 ounces fettuccine
- 1 cup fresh Italian parsley leaves
- ½ cup olive oil
- ¼ cup Parmesan cheese, grated
- ¼ cup pine nuts, plus extra for garnish
- ⅓ cup orange juice
- ¼ cup fresh lemon juice (from 1 lemon)
- ½ teaspoon red pepper flakes, if desired
- Salt and black pepper
- 1 pound shrimp, shelled and deveined (thawed, if frozen)

TIP: Frozen shrimp is a great time-saving ingredient, since it's already shelled and deveined.

1. Cook pasta according to package directions.
2. Meanwhile, in a food processor, combine parsley, oil, cheese, pine nuts, both juices and red pepper flakes; pulse until combined. Season with salt and pepper.
3. In a large skillet set over medium heat, bring citrus sauce to a simmer. Add shrimp; cook 5 minutes, until shrimp are cooked through and no longer translucent.
4. Drain pasta; toss with citrus sauce to coat. Season with salt and pepper. Garnish servings with pine nuts.

Roasted Salmon with Sweet Pepper and Kale Stir-fry

Coating salmon with sesame seeds adds a nutty flavor and crunch to this dish. If you don't have any, skip the egg white coating and cook as directed.

Salmon

- 1 egg white
- 2 tablespoons cornstarch
- 4 salmon fillets (6 ounces each)
- ¼ cup sesame seeds
- 2 teaspoons olive oil

Stir-fry

- 1 tablespoon olive oil
- 1 red pepper, sliced
- 2 teaspoons fresh ginger, peeled and minced
- 1 small bunch (about 8 ounces) kale, trimmed and chopped
- 1 tablespoon reduced-sodium soy sauce
- 2 teaspoons Asian sesame oil
- Salt and black pepper

TIP: Trim off the tough ends and woody center ribs of the kale before chopping.

For salmon:

1. In a small bowl, whisk egg white and cornstarch. Brush the egg white mixture on the skinless side of the salmon; sprinkle with sesame seeds, pressing the seeds to help them adhere.
2. Warm 2 teaspoons oil in a large cast-iron or heavy skillet over medium-high heat. Add salmon fillets; cook 4 minutes per side, until they reach desired doneness.

For stir-fry:

1. Warm 1 tablespoon oil in a large nonstick skillet over medium heat. Add pepper slices and ginger and stir-fry 3 minutes, until softened. Add kale; stir-fry 10 minutes, or until wilted and no longer chewy. Remove from heat; stir in soy sauce and sesame oil. Season to taste with salt and pepper.

Chicken with Mushrooms and White Wine

The savory wine and mushroom sauce takes just 15 minutes to cook, yet tastes as if it took hours.

- 4 boneless, skinless chicken breast halves
- 1 tablespoon olive oil
- 1 tablespoon unsalted butter
- 12 ounces cremini or button mushrooms, sliced
- 1 small onion, diced
- ½ cup white wine
- 1 clove garlic, minced
- ¾ cup reduced-sodium chicken broth
- 2 teaspoons fresh lemon juice
- Salt and black pepper

TIP: Add a pop of color by garnishing the finished dish with chopped parsley.

1. Grill or bake chicken until cooked through.
2. Warm oil and butter in a large nonstick skillet over medium heat. Add mushrooms, onions and wine; cook 8 minutes, stirring. Add garlic; cook 1 minute, stirring. Add broth and bring mixture to a simmer, scraping the bottom of the pan to loosen browned bits. Simmer 5 minutes, to reduce liquid and combine flavors. Add chicken to the skillet; simmer 2 minutes, to warm through.
3. Place chicken on a serving platter. Stir lemon juice, salt and pepper into sauce; pour over chicken.

CHAPTER 2

"Hello, Ana Raquel."

Ana Raquel turned toward the man sitting next to her. She hadn't seen Greg in six years. She could have gone the next sixty without seeing him and been totally happy.

She opened her mouth to tell him that, only suddenly she couldn't speak. Even though he was sitting, she had the sense that he was much taller than she remembered. His shoulders were broader. He seemed so much more like a man than the teenager she remembered from prom night.

His eyes were the same dark brown, as was his hair, and his mouth had a familiar half smile, as if he found her endlessly amusing. Which was probably true, but she doubted he was laughing with her.

"Greg," she managed, despite the fact that her mouth was dry.

"Your street food has everyone talking," he said. "I tried your Curried Chicken Salad over the summer. I like how you mixed in—"

"No, you didn't," she interrupted.

One dark eyebrow rose. "Are you saying I didn't like it or I didn't have it?"

"You didn't have it. You couldn't have. I would have noticed." Having Greg standing in her lunch line would have gotten her attention in a big way.

His expression relaxed and the amused curve returned to his mouth. "I sent a friend. I had a feeling that if I tried to buy something from you, I'd find a frying pan hurtling toward my head."

Ana Raquel felt herself flushing. She stared down at her still twisting fingers. "I would never hurt a paying customer," she murmured.

"I think you'd make an exception for me."

She looked up at him. "I don't dislike you," she told him firmly.

Now both eyebrows rose.

"Not exactly," she added. "It's just . . ."

"Yes?"

"You're so annoying."

Greg surprised her by laughing. The warm, happy sound flowed through her like a sweet, melted ganache. Before she could figure out what to think, let alone what to say, the soft sound of a throat clearing reminded her that they weren't the only ones in the room.

She returned her attention back to the mayor.

"Sorry."

"Not at all." Mayor Marsha smiled at them both. "Greg, I was just telling Ana Raquel that the Fool's Gold cookbook is too big a job for one person. Since you've both thought of it, the obvious solution is for the two of you to work on it together."

She glared at Greg. "You thought of a cookbook, too? One based on home recipes and a few favorites from our restaurants? With some street food thrown in for fun?"

His dark gaze was steady. "Yes. I spoke with the mayor about it last week."

Mayor Marsha nodded in agreement. "Great minds," she said cheerfully.

Right, Ana Raquel thought glumly. Easy for the mayor to be happy. She wasn't the one who had once again been one-upped by Greg Clary.

Ana Raquel glanced at the mayor. She was well and truly trapped. Either she did the cookbook with Greg or she backed out. In which case he would do it on his own. It wasn't the glory that she would miss. It's that she knew exactly how she wanted the book to be. There was no way she was going to let him compromise her vision.

"Fine," she said firmly. "We'll work on it together."

Chapter 3 begins on page 58

sp

Celebrations

Bubbly Feta and Sweet Pepper Dip with Pita Crisps

A cast-iron skillet is the best vessel for this addictive dip—it's ovenproof, so it goes from oven to table.

- 4 tablespoons olive oil
- 1 large onion, thinly sliced
- 3 red peppers, thinly sliced
- 2 tablespoons fresh lemon juice
- 2 tablespoons capers, drained
- ⅓ cup fresh dill or tarragon, chopped
- Salt and black pepper
- 8 ounces goat or feta cheese, crumbled
- Pita crisps, for dipping

TIP: Cooking time will depend on the type of cheese used—you want it to be bubbly but not charred.

1. Warm oil in a medium-heavy ovenproof skillet over low heat. Add onions and peppers; cook 20 minutes, until caramelized and soft, stirring often. Off heat, stir in lemon juice, capers, dill, salt and pepper.
2. Preheat oven to 425°F. Evenly sprinkle cheese over the vegetables. Bake until warmed through and bubbly. Serve with pita crisps.

Toasted Ravioli Bites with Blue Cheese Dipping Sauce

Serve these crispy bites hot
for best taste.

Ravioli bites

- 1 tablespoon whole milk
- 1 large egg
- ½ cup bread crumbs
- ½ package (24½ ounces) fresh or frozen, thawed, spinach-ricotta ravioli
- Vegetable oil

Dipping sauce

- ½ cup mayonnaise
- ½ cup sour cream or plain Greek yogurt
- 2 ounces (about ½ cup) crumbled blue cheese
- 3 tablespoons chopped chives or thinly sliced scallions
- Salt

TIP: You can substitute a jar of blue cheese dressing or marinara sauce for the dipping sauce recipe if you're short on time.

For ravioli bites:

1. Whisk milk and egg in a small bowl. Place bread crumbs in another bowl. Dip ravioli first in egg mixture, then in bread crumbs. Turn to coat.
2. Pour oil into a medium-heavy skillet until it reaches about 1 inch up the sides of the pan. Warm over medium-high heat until a crumb dropped in oil sizzles. Add half of the ravioli; cook about 1 minute per side, until puffed and golden. Using tongs, transfer to a paper towel–lined plate to drain.

For dipping sauce:

1. Whisk mayonnaise and sour cream. Fold in cheese and chives. Season with salt, to taste. Serve with hot ravioli.

Come for Tea Cucumber Salad

This simple recipe is easily expandable for a large group.
Be sure to slice the cucumber super-thin—no need to peel.

Serves 4

- 1 large cucumber, thinly sliced
- 1 pint cherry tomatoes, quartered
- ½ small onion, very thinly sliced
- 1 tablespoon white-wine vinegar
- 1 tablespoon extra-virgin olive oil
- Salt and black pepper
- ¼ cup Parmesan cheese, grated, or feta cheese, crumbled
- 2 tablespoons pine nuts, toasted

TIP: Nothing beats the flavor of fresh tomatoes. In summer, use tomatoes from the farmers' market or your garden. In the off-season, use always-reliable cherry or grape tomatoes.

1. Arrange cucumbers, quartered cherry tomatoes and onions on a large platter. In a small bowl, whisk vinegar and oil; drizzle over salad. Allow to marinate at least 30 minutes. Just before serving, season to taste with salt and pepper and top with cheese and pine nuts.

Farmers' Market Quinoa Salad

Quinoa is a high-fiber, protein-rich grain with a light, nutty flavor. The little round grains cook in 10 minutes, and their tender crunch adds a welcome texture to salads. Cook quinoa until tender but still chewy; you don't want it to get soft.

Serves 4

- 1¾ cups water
- 1 cup quinoa
- Pinch of salt
- 3 tablespoons fresh lemon juice
- 2 tablespoons extra-virgin olive oil
- Salt and black pepper
- 3 scallions, thinly sliced
- 1 small cucumber, peeled and finely diced
- ½ cup carrots, shredded
- 3 tablespoons fresh Italian parsley, finely chopped
- 2 tablespoons fresh mint, finely chopped
- ½ pint cherry tomatoes, preferably a mixture of red and yellow
- ½ cup feta cheese, crumbled

TIP: This recipe serves 4. Feel free to double it.

1. In a small saucepan, bring 1¾ cups water to a boil over high heat. Add quinoa and a pinch of salt; bring back to a boil. Reduce heat to low; cover and simmer 10 minutes, until nearly all the water has been absorbed and the quinoa is tender but not soft.
2. Meanwhile, in a medium bowl, combine lemon juice, oil, salt and pepper. Fold in quinoa, scallions, cucumbers, carrots and herbs. Toss until thoroughly coated. Season with salt and pepper.
3. Thinly slice tomatoes. Arrange on serving plates. Spoon about 1 cup quinoa salad over tomatoes. Garnish with feta.

Celery and Chickpea Salad with Dried Cranberries and Parmesan Dressing

This distinctive and colorful salad
makes an excellent side dish for a spring gathering.

- 3 tablespoons fresh lemon juice
- 2 tablespoons extra-virgin olive oil
- 4 tablespoons Parmesan cheese, grated, plus 4 tablespoons for garnish
- 1 can (15 ounces) chickpeas, drained, rinsed and warmed in microwave
- 8 stalks celery, finely chopped
- ½ cup dried cranberries
- ½ cup roasted almonds, chopped
- 3 ounces baby spinach
- Salt and black pepper

TIP: Tossing the Parmesan dressing with the warm chickpeas helps to blend the flavors and create a dressing for the salad.

1. In a large bowl, whisk lemon juice, oil and Parmesan until a thin paste forms. Fold in warm chickpeas; toss to coat. Fold in celery, cranberries, almonds and spinach. Season to taste with salt and pepper. Garnish with additional Parmesan.

Shaved Fennel Salad with Baby Arugula and Zucchini Ribbons

Slice fennel as thinly as possible—it should be almost translucent. Use a mandolin if you've got one.

- ¼ cup fresh lemon juice
- ¼ cup extra-virgin olive oil
- 2 small fennel bulbs, trimmed and sliced paper-thin
- 1 medium zucchini, very thinly sliced
- ¼ cup fresh dill, chopped
- 3 cups baby arugula (about 2½ ounces)
- Salt and black pepper
- ½ cup pine nuts, toasted

TIP: Zucchini is rarely served raw, but when it's fresh and very thinly sliced, it adds a certain zip to a green salad.

1. In a large serving bowl, whisk lemon juice and oil until blended. Add sliced fennel, zucchini and dill; toss to coat. Let sit 20 minutes.
2. Add arugula; toss to combine. Season to taste with salt and pepper. Garnish with pine nuts.

Asparagus and Spring Green Pasta Salad

A fresh pasta salad, bursting with spring vegetables, will be a big hit at your next picnic.

- 1 pound rotini or penne pasta
- 3 tablespoons olive oil
- 1 pound thin asparagus spears, sliced on the diagonal into 1-inch pieces
- 1½ cups shelled fresh green peas, blanched 1 minute in boiling water, drained, or frozen peas (do not thaw)
- 4 scallions, thinly sliced, white and pale green parts only
- ½ cup Parmesan cheese, finely grated, plus additional for garnish
- ½ cup heavy whipping cream
- 3 tablespoons fresh lemon juice
- 1 tablespoon lemon zest, finely grated
- ½ cup fresh Italian parsley, chopped
- Salt and black pepper

TIP: Remember to zest the lemon before you juice it.

1. Cook pasta according to package directions. Drain, reserving ½ cup of the cooking liquid. Transfer pasta to a large bowl.
2. Warm oil in a large nonstick skillet over medium heat. Add asparagus and cook 3 minutes, stirring. Add peas; cook 2 minutes, until vegetables are crisp-tender. Remove from heat.
3. To pasta in the bowl, fold in vegetable mixture, reserved pasta cooking liquid, scallions, ½ cup Parmesan, cream, lemon juice, lemon zest and parsley. Season to taste with salt, pepper and additional Parmesan.

Roast Leg of Lamb with Spring Herb Pesto and Spinach

Coating leg of lamb with an herb pesto gives it a glossy sheen. After the lamb is cooked, sauté some spinach in all the juices that have settled in the bottom of the pan.

Herb pesto

- ⅓ cup fresh tarragon leaves, packed
- ⅓ cup fresh Italian parsley leaves, packed
- 3 tablespoons olive oil
- 1 tablespoon white-wine vinegar
- 3 cloves garlic
- 2 teaspoons salt
- Water, as needed

Lamb

- 6-pound leg of lamb with bone, well-trimmed and at room temperature
- ½ cup water
- 3 tablespoons pine nuts
- 1 pound spinach, trimmed and coarsely chopped

TIP: It's important to slice off as much of the surface fat from the lamb as possible.

1. Preheat oven to 425°F; position rack in bottom third of oven. In a food processor, pulse tarragon, parsley, oil, vinegar, garlic and salt until a thick paste forms. Add water, a little at a time, and pulse until paste reaches a spreading consistency. Rub pesto over lamb.
2. Set lamb on a rack in a roasting pan; pour about ½ cup of water into the bottom of the pan. Roast for 30 minutes. Reduce oven temperature to 350°F. Roast another 50 minutes, or until an instant-read thermometer inserted in the thickest part registers 135°F for medium-rare. Using tongs, transfer lamb to a carving board; tent loosely with foil and let rest 20 minutes.
3. Pour off all but 2 tablespoons of the fat from the roasting pan; place pan over one or two burners at medium-high heat. Add the pine nuts and spinach; cook until the spinach is tender and the liquid has evaporated. Spoon spinach onto a platter. Carve lamb and arrange slices on top of the spinach.

Spring Festival Cheeseburger Chili

Cheeseburgers and chili in one bowl! Just for fun, serve with hamburger buns for dipping and sopping up every last drop.

1 tablespoon vegetable oil
2 pounds ground chuck
4 tablespoons chili powder
2 teaspoons ground cumin
Salt and black pepper
1 large onion, chopped
2 cloves garlic, chopped
3 cups reduced-sodium beef broth
½ cup ketchup
¼ cup Worcestershire sauce
1 can (15 ounces) red kidney beans, drained

Cheese sauce

2 tablespoons unsalted butter
2 tablespoons all-purpose flour
2 cups whole milk
2 cups cheddar cheese, shredded
Salt and black pepper

Garnishes

Ketchup
Yellow mustard
Red onion, sliced
Corn chips

1. Warm oil in a Dutch oven or a large heavy pot over medium-low heat. Add meat and cook 18 minutes, until browned and nearly dry. Stir in chili powder, cumin, salt and pepper. Add onions and garlic; cook 5 minutes, until softened, stirring. Pour in broth, ketchup and Worcestershire sauce. Bring to a simmer; reduce heat and cook 20 minutes, stirring occasionally. Add beans in the last 5 minutes of cooking.

For cheese sauce:

1. Melt butter in a medium saucepan over low heat. Add flour; stir until incorporated and a paste forms. Slowly pour in milk, a little at a time, stirring with each addition. Let simmer 5 minutes, until thickened, stirring often. Remove from heat; stir in cheese until melted and creamy. Season with salt and pepper.
2. Spoon chili into bowls. Ladle cheese sauce over servings. Drizzle with ketchup, mustard and other garnishes, as desired.

TIP: The chili can be made up to two days in advance. Wait to make the cheese sauce until just before serving.

Spinach and Sun-Dried Tomato Frittata

Frittatas work for breakfast, lunch, tea or dinner. Since they can be served warm or at room temperature, they are a great party food.

- 2 tablespoons olive oil, divided
- ½ small onion, thinly sliced
- 9 ounces baby spinach, coarsely chopped
- 9 large eggs
- ½ cup Parmesan cheese, grated
- ½ cup feta cheese, crumbled
- ½ cup chopped sun-dried tomatoes or roasted red peppers
- Salt and black pepper

TIP: Be sure to use baby spinach, which wilts quickly and doesn't need to be trimmed or chopped.

1. Warm oil in a large nonstick skillet over medium heat. Add onions; cook 3 minutes, stirring. Add chopped spinach; cook 4 minutes, until wilted, stirring.
2. Meanwhile, in a large bowl, whisk eggs until blended. Stir in both cheeses and tomatoes. Season with salt and pepper. Pour egg mixture into skillet, over medium-low heat. Stir to combine. Let sit 1 minute. Using a rubber spatula, lift up mixture around the edges of the pan to let the egg mixture flow underneath; set pan back over heat. Keep doing this until the top is just set, about 5 minutes. Run spatula around the edges of the pan to loosen the frittata; shake pan back and forth to ensure that the frittata is loose in the pan. Pick up the skillet; slide frittata onto a large plate. Place the skillet upside-down over the frittata. Holding the skillet in one hand and the underside of the plate in the other hand, flip the plate so the top of the frittata is now facedown in the skillet. Place the skillet back over medium-low heat. Cook 3 minutes, until eggs are set.
3. Run spatula around the edges of the frittata to loosen it from the pan; slide it onto the platter. Serve warm or at room temperature.

Savory Ricotta and Leek Pie

This is a foolproof make-ahead side dish for Easter dinner. Since it calls for premade pie crust, it's also super-easy.

- 2 tablespoons unsalted butter
- 2 medium leeks (about 1 pound), trimmed, cleaned and very thinly sliced
- 1 cup cooked bacon, chopped, optional
- 1½ teaspoons fresh thyme, chopped, plus additional for garnish
- Salt
- 8 ounces (just under 1 cup) ricotta cheese, preferably fresh
- 1 large egg
- ½ cup heavy cream
- ⅓ cup whole milk
- 1 prepared 9-inch pie crust

TIP: For meat-lovers, stir into the leeks a cup of chopped, cooked bacon to add a punch of meaty, salty flavor. Want even more flavor? Sprinkle the pie with grated Parmesan before baking.

1. Melt butter in a large nonstick skillet over medium-low heat. Add leeks; cook 12 minutes, until golden and tender, stirring often. Add bacon, if desired. Remove from heat; stir in thyme and salt.
2. Preheat oven to 400°F. In a large bowl, whisk ricotta, egg, cream and milk. Fold in leek mixture. Scrape mixture into the pie crust and bake 30 to 35 minutes, until just set and golden. Serve warm or at room temperature.

Chipotle Chicken Taco Bake

Make taco night festive by serving the tacos nestled in a bed of yellow rice.

Serves 4

- 1 package (10 ounces) Spanish or Mexican rice blend
- 1 tablespoon olive oil
- ½ red onion, diced
- 2 cloves garlic, chopped
- ½ teaspoon ground cumin
- ½ teaspoon ground coriander
- Salt and black pepper
- 1 canned chipotle chili in adobo sauce, seeded and minced
- 1 cup canned tomatoes, diced
- 2 cups cooked chicken, shredded
- 8 taco shells
- 1 can (15 ounces) black beans, drained and rinsed
- ¾ cup cheddar cheese, shredded

Garnishes

- Sour cream
- Avocado, diced
- Fresh cilantro, chopped

TIP: If chipotle chilies aren't available, substitute a chopped jalapeño pepper.

1. Preheat oven to 400°F. Prepare rice according to package directions. Retain in the covered cooking pot to keep warm.
2. Meanwhile, warm oil in a large ovenproof skillet. Add onions; cook 6 minutes, until softened, stirring often. Add garlic, cumin, coriander, salt and pepper; cook 30 seconds, stirring. Stir in chili, tomatoes and chicken; cook until warmed through. Transfer mixture to a bowl.
3. Spoon cooked rice mixture into the same skillet (no need to clean). Spoon the chicken mixture evenly into the taco shells; top with beans and cheese. Nestle tacos into the rice mixture. Place skillet in the oven and bake for 10 minutes, until the cheese melts and the dish is hot. Serve with garnishes.

Chopped Chicken Cobb Salad

A perfect option for a springtime dinner party: a make-ahead, main-dish salad.

Serves 6

Dressing

- ¼ cup extra-virgin olive oil
- 2 tablespoons sherry or red-wine vinegar
- 1 tablespoon fresh lemon juice
- ¼ teaspoon Dijon mustard
- ¼ teaspoon Worcestershire sauce
- ¼ teaspoon granulated sugar
- 1 clove garlic, minced
- Salt and black pepper
- 2 tablespoons fresh chives, chopped

Salad

- 6 strips bacon
- 4 boneless, skinless chicken breast halves
- Salt and black pepper
- 1 small head iceberg lettuce, chopped
- 1 bunch watercress, trimmed and chopped
- 3 hard-boiled eggs, diced
- 2 medium tomatoes, diced
- 1 avocado, diced
- 2 ounces blue cheese, or another favorite cheese

For dressing:

1. In a medium bowl, preferably one with a spout, whisk all dressing ingredients until well blended.

For salad:

1. In a large heavy skillet, cook bacon until crisp. Transfer the bacon to a paper towel–lined plate to drain; crumble. Drain most of the drippings from the skillet; place the skillet on medium-high heat. Season chicken with salt and pepper; add to pan and cook 6 minutes per side, until cooked through. Let cool slightly; cut into cubes.
2. On a large platter, toss lettuce, watercress and about half the dressing to coat. Arrange chicken, bacon and all remaining salad ingredients on top of the lettuce, setting them in rows. Just before serving, drizzle the remaining dressing over the entire salad.

TIP: Use extra-virgin olive oil for uncooked dishes, when you can really taste the oil. In cooked dishes, less expensive regular pressed oil is fine.

Strawberry-Rhubarb Crumble Bars

These bars feature a rich shortbread base, a sweet-tart fruit layer and a crunchy crumb topping. They make great picnic or bake sale fare.

Filling

- 1 medium rhubarb stalk (about ¾ pound), thinly sliced
- ⅓ cup granulated sugar
- 1 tablespoon cornstarch
- Cinnamon stick
- 1 pint strawberries, hulled and quartered

Crust

- 2 cups all-purpose flour
- ½ cup light-brown sugar
- ½ teaspoon salt
- 12 tablespoons (1½ sticks) unsalted butter, at room temperature, cut into 8 pieces, plus additional to grease the foil

Crumble

- ¾ cup old-fashioned oats
- ½ cup all-purpose flour
- ½ cup light-brown sugar
- ½ cup walnuts, chopped
- 1 teaspoon ground cinnamon
- Pinch of salt
- 4 tablespoons (½ stick) unsalted butter, at room temperature, cut into 8 pieces

For filling:

1. In a medium saucepan, combine rhubarb, sugar and cornstarch. Let it sit 10 minutes to release juices. Add the cinnamon stick and bring to a boil over medium-high heat. Reduce heat; simmer 8 minutes, until softened. Remove from heat; let cool slightly. Stir in strawberries.

For crust:

1. Meanwhile, preheat oven to 350°F. Line a 9-inch-square baking pan with foil; grease foil. In a food processor, pulse flour, brown sugar and salt. Add butter; pulse until mixture comes together. Press dough evenly into the prepared pan. Bake 25 minutes, until lightly golden. Transfer to a wire rack. Spread filling over crust.

For crumble:

1. In a medium bowl, combine oats, flour, brown sugar, walnuts, cinnamon and salt. Add butter chunks and mix with your fingers or a fork until mixture holds together in pea-sized chunks. Sprinkle evenly over filling. Bake 25 to 30 minutes, until crumble is crispy and fruit is bubbling. Cool on a wire rack.

TIP: If you use frozen rhubarb, make sure to thaw and thoroughly drain it.

Lattice-Top Peach Pie

You'll be the talk of the town when you bring this luscious—and gorgeous—peach pie to the church social or your company picnic.

Double crust

- 2½ cups all-purpose flour
- 1 tablespoon granulated sugar, plus additional for sprinkling on crust
- Pinch of salt
- 1 cup (2 sticks) unsalted butter, cold and cut into cubes
- ¼–½ cup cold water, as needed
- Milk, for baking
- Granulated sugar, for baking

TIP: For even baking, use an all-glass pie plate. Its angled sides prevent crusts from sliding down and it neatly fits store-bought crusts as well.

Filling

- 6 large, ripe peaches, peeled and thinly sliced
- ⅓ cup granulated sugar
- ⅓ cup brown sugar
- Pinch of ground cinnamon
- Pinch of ground nutmeg
- Pinch of salt
- 2 tablespoons cornstarch

Lattice-Top Peach Pie

Recipe continued from previous page.

For crust:

1. In a food processor, pulse flour, sugar and salt until combined. Add butter; pulse until mixture resembles wet sand. Slowly add cold water, a little at a time, just until dough comes together into a craggy mass. Turn dough out onto a floured countertop; divide dough in half. Form each half into a thick disk; wrap in plastic and refrigerate at least 1 hour or up to 2 days.
2. Remove dough from the refrigerator about 20 minutes before rolling out. Using a floured rolling pin, roll out 1 disk on a lightly floured countertop to a 12-inch circle. Transfer to a glass pie tin. Press dough to fit the tin; flute edges. Refrigerate the crust in the pie tin while making the filling.

For filling:

1. Preheat oven to 400°F. In a large bowl, combine peaches, both sugars, cinnamon, nutmeg, salt and cornstarch until evenly coated.
2. Remove crust from refrigerator; spread filling into the chilled crust. Using the same method as in step 2 of crust directions, roll out the second crust to a 12-inch round. Cut the round into 1-inch strips. Place half the strips in one direction over the filling, spaced evenly apart. Place the remaining strips going the other direction, weaving them under and over the first set of strips to make a lattice. The strips should stop at the top crimped edges, not go over them. Brush the lattice and crust edges with milk and sprinkle with granulated sugar.
3. Place the pie on a baking sheet; bake 20 minutes. Reduce heat to 350°F; bake 45 minutes, until crust is browned and fruit is bubbling. Remove to a wire rack to cool. Let the pie cool at least 2 hours, for filling to set, before serving.

TIP: For a special sparkly finish, sprinkle the top of the pie with large-grained, or sanding, sugar before baking.

Chewy Chocolate Chip Cookies

Do you really need another chocolate chip cookie recipe? You do if you've been searching for a cookie that's perfectly crisp around the edges, yet rich and chewy in the middle.

Makes about 32

- 4 cups all-purpose flour
- 1¼ teaspoons baking soda
- 1½ teaspoons baking powder
- 1 teaspoon salt
- 1¼ cups (2½ sticks) unsalted butter, at room temperature
- 1¼ cups light-brown sugar
- 1 cup granulated sugar
- 2 large eggs
- 1 tablespoon pure vanilla extract
- 3½ cups (18 ounces) semisweet chocolate chips

TIP: Refrigerating the dough for at least 24 hours helps to make the cookie extra-chewy. The dough will feel dry, but that lack of moisture improves the baked texture.

1. In a bowl, whisk flour, baking soda, baking powder and salt until blended.
2. In a large bowl with an electric mixer on high speed, cream butter and both sugars until light and fluffy. Add eggs, one at a time, beating well after each addition. Beat in vanilla. Reduce mixer speed to low, add dry ingredients and beat just until blended. Remove from mixer; fold in chips. Cover bowl and refrigerate 24 hours, or up to 72 hours.
3. Preheat oven to 350°F. Line 2 baking sheets with parchment paper or nonstick baking pads. Drop dough in golf ball–sized mounds onto prepared sheets. Press down on balls with your palm to flatten slightly. Bake, 1 sheet at a time, for 12 minutes, or until golden around the edges but still slightly wet in the middle. Let cool 5 minutes on the pan. Transfer cookies to a wire rack to cool completely.

Tiny Lemon Cakes

Cake

- 1½ cups plus 2 tablespoons all-purpose flour, plus additional for pan
- ¼ teaspoon baking powder
- Pinch of salt
- ½ cup (1 stick) unsalted butter, cut into 8 pieces, plus additional for greasing pan
- 1½ cups granulated sugar
- 3 large eggs
- ½ cup sour cream
- ¼ teaspoon pure lemon extract
- 1 tablespoon lemon peel, grated
- 2 teaspoons fresh lemon juice

Glaze and decoration

- 1 cup powdered sugar
- 3 tablespoons fresh lemon juice
- Silver dragees

TIP: The FDA recommends that silver dragees be used for decoration only.

Elegant, sweet and beautiful.
Perfect for a tea party or as a hostess gift.

For cake:

1. Preheat oven to 350°F. Grease and lightly flour an 8-inch loaf pan. In a bowl, whisk flour, baking powder and salt.
2. In a large bowl with an electric mixer on high speed, cream butter and sugar until light and blended. Add eggs, one at a time, beating well after each addition. Scrape down the sides of the bowl.
3. In a glass measuring cup, whisk sour cream, lemon extract, peel and juice until blended. Alternately, add dry ingredients and sour cream mixture to the butter mixture; beat just until blended. Do not overmix.
4. Scrape dough into prepared pan. Bake 55 minutes, until a toothpick inserted in center comes out clean. Transfer to a wire rack; let cool 15 minutes in the pan. Run a knife around the outside of the cake to loosen it from the pan. Invert the cake onto a wire rack to cool completely, preferably overnight.

For glaze:

1. In a bowl, whisk powdered sugar and lemon juice until of drizzling consistency.

To serve:

1. Slice cooled cake into 1-inch-thick slices. Lay slices flat on the counter. Using a 1-inch-round cookie cutter, cut tiny cakes out of the slices, staying away from the browned edges of each slice. (Save the edges for snacking.) Set cakes on a wire rack. Drizzle glaze over the cakes until coated. Dot with silver dragees.

Strawberry Shortcakes

Nothing says spring like strawberry shortcake. Be sure to let the strawberries rest, or macerate, in sugar, in order to create the lovely sweet strawberry syrup.

Shortcakes

- 2 cups plus 2 tablespoons all-purpose flour
- ½ cup cake flour
- 1 tablespoon baking powder
- ¼ cup granulated sugar, plus additional to sprinkle on biscuits before baking
- ½ teaspoon salt
- ½ cup (1 stick) cold unsalted butter, cut into cubes
- 1 cup cold buttermilk
- Heavy cream, to brush on biscuits before baking

Filling

- 2 pints strawberries, washed, hulled and sliced
- ¼ cup granulated sugar
- 1½ cups heavy cream, whipped, for garnish

TIP: For the lightest cakes, handle he dough as little as possible.

For shortcakes:

1. Preheat oven to 425°F. Line a large baking sheet with parchment paper or a nonstick baking pad.
2. In a food processor, pulse both flours, baking powder, sugar and salt until blended. Add cold butter; pulse until mixture resembles coarse meal. Add buttermilk; pulse until dough forms a moist ball.
3. Scrape dough onto a lightly floured countertop. Knead a few times; pat into a ¾-inch high circle. Using a 2- to 3-inch biscuit cutter, cut out 10 biscuits. Push any scraps together to form additional biscuits, if desired. Transfer to prepared sheets. Lightly brush with cream; sprinkle with sugar.
4. Bake 15 to 20 minutes, until golden. Let cool 5 minutes on baking sheet. Transfer to a wire rack.

For filling:

1. In a large bowl, combine sliced strawberries and sugar. Toss to coat; let sit 30 minutes, until strawberries release their liquid. In a large bowl with an electric mixer or whisk, whip cream.

To serve:

1. Slice biscuits in half horizontally. Place bottom half on dessert plate; top with a spoonful of strawberries and whipped cream. Top with the top half of the biscuit. Add another scoop of cream; drizzle with juice from the strawberry bowl. Serve immediately.

Birthday Party Banana Layer Cake

Cake

- 2⅔ cups all-purpose flour, plus additional for pans
- 1 tablespoon baking powder
- ½ teaspoon baking soda
- ½ teaspoon salt
- 1 cup (2 sticks) unsalted butter, at room temperature, plus additional for greasing pans
- 2 cups granulated sugar
- 4 large eggs
- 3 very ripe bananas, chopped
- 1 tablespoon pure vanilla extract
- ½ cup buttermilk

Frosting

- 8 ounces cream cheese, at room temperature
- 6 tablespoons unsalted butter, at room temperature
- 4 cups powdered sugar
- 1 teaspoon vanilla extract
- Pinch of salt
- Pecan halves, for garnish

TIP: The riper the banana, the deeper the flavor.

There's something springy about a light, fruit-flavored cake.
This one is super-rich, so make the slices small.

For cake:

1. Preheat oven to 350°F. Grease and flour the bottom and sides of two 9-inch cake pans.
2. In a medium bowl, whisk flour, baking powder, baking soda and salt until combined.
3. In a large bowl with an electric mixer on high speed, beat butter and sugar until light and fluffy, about 3 minutes. Add the eggs, one at a time, beating well after each addition. Add bananas and vanilla extract; beat until blended. (Mixture will look curdled—don't worry.) Reduce mixer speed to low, and alternately add dry ingredients and buttermilk, beginning and ending with dry ingredients.
4. Pour batter into prepared pans. Bake 35 to 40 minutes, until a toothpick inserted in the center comes out clean. Let the cake cool in the pans for 10 minutes. Run a knife around the sides of the cakes to loosen from the pans. Invert layers onto wire racks to cool completely.

For frosting:

1. In a large bowl with an electric mixer on high speed, beat cream cheese and butter until smooth. Add powdered sugar, vanilla and salt; beat until fluffy.
2. Brush away any loose crumbs from the cooled cake. Place 1 layer on a cake plate; top with about 1 cup frosting. Using a metal spatula, spread the frosting over the layer. Place the second layer, top-side down, on top of the frosting. Spread a thin layer of frosting over the entire cake to seal in crumbs. Frost the remaining cake. Arrange pecan halves around the top rim of the cake.

CHAPTER 3

Ana Raquel and Greg walked out to the City Hall parking lot. She was hoping to come up with a brilliant reason why he couldn't help her with the cookbook project, but nothing came to mind. When they reached their cars—hers, a beat-up old pickup and his, a shiny new blue SUV—she decided to accept the inevitable but try to stay in control of the situation.

"We should get together and discuss how we're going to approach the cookbook," she told him. "I have a lot of ideas."

He nodded. "Me, too. I've already spoken to Colleen at the *Fool's Gold Daily Republic*."

"Why would you talk to the newspaper editor?"

"I thought she might want to have someone write a story on what we're doing. We could get input from the community."

"That makes sense," Ana Raquel murmured. She'd been thinking of putting up a few flyers, asking for recipe submissions, but an article in the local paper was more efficient and a good calling card. While the rest of the world had gone digital to get its news, here in Fool's Gold, the daily paper was still alive and well. One of the advantages of small-town living, she supposed.

"I know a lot of families have recipes that have been passed down for generations," she said. "Those would be fun to go through."

"You're going to include your grandmother's fried chicken recipe, aren't you?"

She stared at him. "How do you know about that?"

He grinned. "Your mom invited the whole student council over for dinner one year. That's what she served. She told us how her mom had taught her to make it and how she'd taught you."

Ana Raquel remembered the evening very well. Her parents had found Greg oh-so-charming and didn't understand why she was upset that he'd defeated her for the student council presidency. She was surprised that he would recall something as simple as a fried chicken dinner.

"I was planning on putting that one in the cookbook," she said slowly.

"Good." He flashed her another smile. "I've been trying to duplicate the recipe myself, but I don't have it right. Now I can find out what ingredient I've been leaving out."

He was being so nice, she thought, confused by his friendliness. She had always thought they were sworn enemies. Or at least people who didn't get along. How embarrassing that she seemed to be the only one showing up for the fight.

"Are you free Monday?" he asked. "The restaurant is closed. We can meet at my place."

She was suddenly curious about where Greg lived. "Your place would be great. I serve lunch until two-thirty. So say four?"

He nodded and gave her his address. "Great. I'll prepare us a little something and we can get to work on the cookbook. See you then."

He got in his SUV and drove away. Ana Raquel was left standing in the parking lot with the growing sense that Greg was not who she remembered at all.

Chapter 4 begins on page 61

CHAPTER 4

Greg lived on the edge of the Condor Valley Winery. Ana Raquel parked next to his SUV, then circled around the side of the house to take in the views from the backyard. To the south and west were the vineyards. They were thick and lush with heavy grapes. She didn't know much about making wine, but she was pretty sure the harvest would start in a few weeks.

To the east were the mountains of the Sierra Nevada. In the winter, they would be covered with snow. Fortunately, the town was high enough to get a little snow, but it rarely got more than a few inches at a time. With the mountains so close, you could get all the thrill without so much of the hassle.

She turned her attention to the house. It was a cabin-style one-story. Small, but appealing. There were probably a couple of bedrooms and a single bath. Enough space for one person, she thought. Greg wasn't married. He was—

Ana Raquel started toward the house, only to stop suddenly. The local rumor mill was quite efficient and she heard most of what was going on. But knowing that Greg wasn't married was different from knowing if he were dating someone. Not that she was interested for herself, it was just that if he had a girlfriend, the cookbook project could be even more complicated. There would be long evenings and weekends perfecting recipes. Arguments about style and placement. She didn't want some nonfoodie offering her opinion because she was being protective of her boyfriend.

In fact, if Greg were seeing someone, there was simply no way this project could work, she thought as she marched around the house and up the front steps. She would tell him that and he could back out. Then she would do it all herself, which would be just fine. Because she wasn't interested in working with a guy who dated a girl like that. Someone so possessive and willing to stick her nose in where it didn't belong.

The front door opened and the man in question smiled at her.

"Hey," he said. "Right on time. Come on in."

She did as he requested, trying not to let him know that her tummy suddenly felt weird and she couldn't say why. There were flutterings and odd zings of electricity. Had she eaten some bad fish?

"Hi." She stepped past him and shrugged out of her coat. "Great place. So is it all yours? What about a roommate? A girlfriend? Because working with you is one thing, but working with a cast of thousands isn't possible."

His dark gaze settled on her face. "I don't have a girlfriend."

"Oh. Are you sure? Because you always did. Constantly. It was a steady stream of women."

That half smile appeared. "I've grown up since then."

An intriguing statement that told her exactly nothing, she thought in frustration. Which was just so like him.

Determined not to give him the satisfaction of asking or acting as if she cared, she dropped her coat and bag on the bench in the foyer and walked into the small house.

The view from the living room stretched all the way to the end of the valley, but what really caught her attention was the huge kitchen. She stumbled toward it, drawn by deep sinks, plenty of counter space and a six-burner stove. There were two ovens, a warming drawer and a knife collection that nearly had her drooling with envy.

"Wow," she said, turning in a slow circle. "I mean wow."

There were racks and lots of cabinets and a double pantry. To the left, one section of countertop was done in marble. The cool, smooth surface was perfect for rolling out dough and making cookies. Through the glass door of the top oven, she saw a rotisserie. While she loved her little trailer kitchen, comparing this to that was like comparing truffle oil to cooking spray.

Greg leaned against the doorframe, his broad shoulders filling the space. "I did some remodeling before I moved in. I still have to get to the bathroom."

"Who cares about a bathroom?" she told him. "Or furniture. For a kitchen like this, I would be willing to sit on crates and sleep on the floor."

"No need for that. I have a bed."

A comment that caused the fluttering inside to increase for a second before she decided to ignore the sensation.

He pushed off the doorframe and walked toward the dining alcove. She saw that he'd placed a couple of folders and an open bottle of wine on the butcher block table.

"Shall we?" he asked, holding out a chair.

4

"Sure."

She took the seat he offered, then nodded when he held up the wine bottle. Maybe sipping the excellent cabernet would settle her nerves. It wasn't that she was nervous, she told herself. This was a new situation—that was all. She was being forced to share her dream. That would be uncomfortable for anyone. Her fluttery tummy had nothing to do with being around Greg.

He sat across from her and picked up his glass of wine. "To the Fool's Gold Cookbook," he said, touching his glass to hers.

Before she could respond, he chuckled.

"What?" she asked.

"I can't believe we're doing this. After all these years." He shrugged. "I still remember the first time I saw you. We'd just moved to town. I was seven and I didn't know anyone. My mom told me I should sign up for the second-grade play as a way to make new friends. I walked into tryouts and there you were. All blond curls and big eyes."

He sipped his wine. "I went home and told my mother I'd fallen in love."

Ana Raquel felt herself blink. "With me?"

"Yup. When I was picked to be Prince Charming, I knew it was meant to be." He smiled again. "Of course, I was only seven."

Chapter 5 begins on page 88

sum

Warm Weather Meals

Grilled Cheese, Pear and Prosciutto Sandwiches

This is a sophisticated version of the classic grilled cheese sandwich. The clever cooking technique means you can make sandwiches for the whole family all at the same time.

- 8 slices challah or other firm white bread
- 4 tablespoons unsalted butter, at room temperature
- 8 ounces Jarlsberg or fontina cheese, thinly sliced
- 4 large slices prosciutto
- 1 ripe pear, sliced

TIP: Bartlett pears are a good choice—just make sure they're ripe.

1. Preheat oven to 425°F. Place two rimmed baking sheets in the oven to warm for at least 10 minutes.
2. Spread 1 side of 4 bread slices with a thin layer of butter. Carefully lay slices, buttered-side down, onto one hot baking sheet. Top evenly with cheese, prosciutto and pear slices. Top with remaining bread. Spread remaining butter on top of those bread slices; place second hot baking sheet over the sandwiches, rim side up. Place "sandwich" of baking sheets in oven. Bake 6 minutes, until cheese is melted and bread golden. Carefully remove the hot baking sheets; transfer sandwiches to cutting board.

End-of-Summer Tomato Tart

Don't think twice about making this tart crust—you whip it up in the food processor in seconds, then just press it into the tart pan. Serve this elegant tart with a crisp green salad and, for heartier appetites, grilled sausage.

Crust

- 1½ cups unbleached all-purpose flour
- Pinch of salt
- 6 tablespoons cold unsalted butter, chopped
- 1 large egg
- 2–3 tablespoons cold water

Filling

- ⅓ cup crème fraiche
- 1 teaspoon Dijon mustard
- 2 medium heirloom or beefsteak tomatoes
- Salt and black pepper
- 6 ounces fresh mozzarella cheese, sliced into thin rounds
- 2 tablespoons fresh basil, chopped

TIP: The crème fraiche–mustard base guards against a soggy crust and adds a creamy bite.

For crust:

1. In a food processor, pulse flour and salt until combined. Add butter and egg; pulse until dough forms tiny balls. Add water, a tablespoon at a time, just until dough holds together when you pinch it with your fingers. Scrape dough out of the bowl and shape it into a disk. Wrap disk in plastic; flatten slightly and refrigerate for at least 30 minutes and up to 24 hours.
2. Preheat oven to 425°F. Press dough into and up the sides of a 9-inch tart pan, either metal or ceramic.

For filling:

1. In a small bowl, whisk crème fraiche and mustard until blended. Evenly spread this mixture over the dough. Thinly slice tomatoes. Using a small spoon or your fingers, carefully remove as many of the seeds as possible and wet pulp from the middle of the slices. Arrange slices in tart; season with salt and pepper. Randomly top with mozzarella slices. Bake 30 minutes, until crust is golden and cheese is bubbling. Sprinkle tart with basil.

Summer Garden Wheatberry Salad

Wheatberries are a hearty, fiber-rich grain that have a chewy, satisfying bite. If wheatberries are unavailable, you can substitute barley, brown rice or wild rice, cooked according to package directions.

- 1 cup wheatberries
- 3 cups water, plus extra as needed
- 3 tablespoons extra-virgin olive oil
- 3 tablespoons sherry or red-wine vinegar
- 1 small cucumber, peeled, seeded and diced
- ½ pint cherry tomatoes, halved
- 1 teaspoon salt
- 1 small shallot, minced
- ½ cup black olives, chopped
- ½ cup fresh Italian parsley, chopped
- 1 cup goat cheese (about 4 ounces), crumbled

TIP: For best flavor, toss wheatberries with oil and vinegar while still warm.

1. In a medium saucepan, combine wheatberries with 3 cups water. Bring to a boil; reduce heat and simmer 45 minutes until soft but still chewy, adding water as needed. Drain; scrape into a large bowl, toss with oil and vinegar and let cool.
2. Set a colander in the sink; add cucumber, tomatoes, and salt; toss to coat. Let stand 15 minutes.
3. Add drained cucumber and tomatoes, shallots, olives and parsley to the wheatberries in the bowl. Fold in goat cheese; season with salt.

Memorial Day Chicken Salad

This is a perfect no-cook meal for a busy night. Ingredient amounts given are guidelines—feel free to alter them as you assemble the salad.

- ¼ cup mayonnaise, or as much as desired
- 1 tablespoon fresh lemon juice
- 1 cup cooked chicken, chopped
- ¼ cup cheddar cheese, shredded
- 2 tablespoons pecans, chopped
- 1 small carrot, shredded
- 2 tablespoons fresh chives, chopped
- Salt and black pepper
- 2 big handfuls baby salad greens

TIP: Chives and scallions are often used in salads because they are milder members of the onion family.

1. In a medium bowl, whisk mayonnaise and lemon juice until combined. Fold in chicken, cheese, pecans, carrots and chives. Season with salt and pepper.
2. Line two serving plates with salad greens; mound chicken salad on the greens.

Curried Chicken Salad

If you've got leftover chicken, or you pick up a rotisserie chicken at the market, you can assemble this deli-style salad in just a few minutes.

- ¼ cup mayonnaise
- 2 tablespoons plain yogurt or sour cream
- 1 tablespoon fresh lemon or lime juice
- 1 teaspoon curry powder
- ¼ teaspoon ground cumin
- 2 cooked chicken breast halves, shredded
- 2 scallions, thinly sliced
- Salt and black pepper
- 2 cups chopped crisp lettuce, such as romaine
- ½ cup sugar snap peas, halved and blanched
- 1 cup red grapes, halved
- ⅓ cup cashews, coarsely chopped

TIP: To blanch snap peas, add them to a pot of boiling water for 2 minutes, drain and rinse them in cool water.

1. In a medium bowl, whisk mayonnaise, yogurt, lemon juice, curry and cumin. Fold in shredded chicken and scallions. Season with salt and pepper.
2. Line 2 serving plates with lettuce, peas and grapes. Add a scoop of chicken salad to each plate; garnish with cashews.

Caramelized Onion, White Bean and Wilted Arugula Crostini

Cooking onions for a long time over low heat brings out their sweetness, which is a perfect complement to mellow beans and sharp arugula. Serve with a crisp green salad for a light supper.

- 3 tablespoons pine nuts
- 2 tablespoons olive oil, divided
- 2 large yellow onions, thinly sliced
- Salt and black pepper
- 2 teaspoons fresh rosemary, chopped
- 1 can (15 ounces) white kidney or cannellini beans, drained and rinsed
- 3 cups (about 2½ ounces) baby arugula leaves
- 4 thick slices whole-grain bread

TIP: When caramelizing onions, keep the heat very low and keep stirring. You want the onions to be a light golden brown, not burned. Drizzle in a bit more oil if onions are overbrowning.

1. Warm a large nonstick skillet over low heat. Add pine nuts; toast 1 minute, until lightly browned, stirring. Remove pine nuts from the skillet.
2. Warm 1 tablespoon of the oil in the same skillet over medium-low heat. Add onions; cook 5 minutes, stirring. Reduce heat to very low; cover pot and let cook 25 minutes, until onions are very tender and golden, stirring often. Season with salt, pepper and rosemary. Increase heat to medium; stir in beans and arugula. Cook until beans are warmed through and arugula wilts, stirring. Add a tablespoon or two of water if the mixture becomes too sticky.
3. Meanwhile, preheat oven to 350°F. Place bread slices on a baking sheet, brush with the remaining tablespoon of oil and bake 10 minutes, until toasted. Top each toast with some of the onion mixture; garnish with toasted pine nuts.

Ten-Minute Crisp Chopped Salad

Vibrant, crunchy and super-healthy,
this salad works as a light dinner or a quick side dish.

Serves 4

- 1 medium cucumber, peeled, halved, seeded and finely diced
- 1½ cups halved cherry or pear tomatoes (about ¾ of a pint container)
- Salt and black pepper
- 3 tablespoons extra-virgin olive oil
- 2 tablespoons white-wine vinegar
- 1 small clove garlic, minced
- 1 can (14 ounces) chickpeas, drained and rinsed
- 1 cup mushrooms, sliced
- ½ cup fresh flat-leaf parsley, tarragon or dill, chopped
- 3 cups iceberg or romaine lettuce, chopped
- 1 cup feta cheese (about 4 ounces), crumbled

TIP: Salting, then draining the cucumber and tomatoes before tossing them with the other ingredients releases their liquid so they don't make the salad soggy.

1. Set a colander in the sink; add cucumber, tomatoes and 1 teaspoon salt; toss to coat. Let stand 10 minutes.
2. In a large serving bowl, whisk oil, vinegar and garlic until combined. Add chickpeas, mushrooms and parsley; toss to coat. Add cucumber mixture; toss again.
3. Just before serving, toss in lettuce and cheese. Season with salt and pepper.

Heidi's Arugula, Corn and Tomato Salad with Goat Cheese

When the corn is super-fresh, there's no need to cook it.
This salad is a great accompaniment to grilled fish or chicken.

- 3 tablespoons extra-virgin olive oil
- 1 tablespoon balsamic vinegar
- 1 tablespoon fresh lemon juice
- 1 small clove garlic, minced
- Salt and black pepper
- 4 ounces baby arugula (about 5 handfuls)
- 2 ears corn, kernels scraped off
- 1 large tomato, chopped
- ¼ cup fresh basil, chopped
- 1 cup goat cheese, crumbled

TIP: Use a serrated knife to scrape the kernels off the corn.

1. In a large serving bowl, whisk oil, vinegar, lemon juice, garlic, salt and pepper until blended. Add arugula, corn, tomatoes and basil; toss to coat. Top with goat cheese and serve immediately.

Caprese Pasta Salad with Balsamic Chicken

This is another one of those versatile dishes that can be served warm, cold or at room temperature.

Chicken

- 3 boneless, skinless chicken breast halves (about 1½ pounds)
- 3 tablespoons balsamic vinegar
- 2 tablespoons fresh lemon juice
- 1 tablespoon Dijon mustard
- 3 cloves garlic, minced
- Salt and black pepper

Pasta salad

- 3 tablespoons extra-virgin olive oil
- 1 tablespoon fresh lemon juice
- 1 small shallot, minced
- Salt and black pepper
- 1½ pounds ripe beefsteak or heirloom tomatoes
- 12 ounces fresh mozzarella, cut into ½-inch cubes
- 1 pound fusilli or gemelli pasta
- ½ cup fresh basil

TIP: Remember that tomatoes taste best if stored at room temperature—only refrigerate them if they've been cut.

For chicken:

1. In a resealable bag, combine chicken and all marinade ingredients. Seal bag; turn to coat chicken. Marinate, refrigerated, for at least 30 minutes or up to 24 hours.

For pasta salad:

1. In a large serving bowl, whisk oil, lemon juice, shallots, salt and pepper. Fold in tomatoes and mozzarella cubes; let sit for at least 15 minutes or up to 45 minutes.
2. Cook pasta according to package directions. Drain; rinse with cool water.
3. Meanwhile, remove chicken from marinade. (Discard marinade.) Grill chicken until cooked through. (Alternatively, chicken could be cooked on the stovetop for about 6 minutes per side.) Transfer to a cutting board. Let stand 10 minutes; thinly slice.
4. Add pasta, chicken and basil to tomato mixture; toss gently to combine.

Green Pasta Pesto with Zucchini Carpaccio

Spinach adds bright green color and a blast of vitamins to this pasta sauce. Serve pasta warm, cold or at room temperature.

Serves 4–6

- 2 cups basil leaves, packed
- 1 cup fresh spinach leaves
- ⅓–½ cup extra-virgin olive oil, as needed
- ½ cup Parmesan cheese, grated
- 2 tablespoons pine nuts
- Salt
- 1 pound penne or fusilli pasta
- 1 large zucchini, very thinly sliced
- 1 pint cherry tomatoes, halved

TIP: Pesto can be made 2 days in advance. Store, tightly covered, in the refrigerator.

1. In a food processor, combine basil, spinach, ⅓ cup oil, cheese, pine nuts and 1 teaspoon salt. Process until puréed. Add additional oil, if needed.
2. Meanwhile, cook pasta according to package directions. In a large bowl, toss zucchini slices with ½ teaspoon salt in a colander set in the sink. Let drain 15 minutes, shaking colander occasionally.
3. In a serving bowl, toss warm pasta with pesto sauce. Let pasta cool. Before serving, add zucchini slices and tomatoes. Season to taste with salt.

Buttery Tilapia with Dijon Dill Green Beans

You don't need to worry about the timing for this meal. The beans can be served warm or at room temperature. And the tilapia is a flash in the pan—it cooks in the time it takes to set the table!

Beans

1 pound green beans, trimmed

2 teaspoons Dijon mustard

2 teaspoons white-wine vinegar

3 tablespoons extra-virgin olive oil

Salt and black pepper

2 tablespoons fresh dill, chopped

Tilapia

1 tablespoon unsalted butter

1 tablespoon olive oil

Four 6-ounce tilapia fillets, halved lengthwise to fit in pan

Salt and black pepper

TIP: Use only fresh dill in this recipe. Dried dill doesn't impart the same flavor.

For beans:

1. Using a steamer, steam beans until crisp-tender, about 6 minutes. Drain and rinse in cold water. Meanwhile, in a large serving bowl, whisk mustard, vinegar, oil, salt and pepper until blended. Add beans and dill to bowl; toss until coated.

For tilapia:

1. Warm butter and oil in a large nonstick skillet over medium-high heat. Season tilapia with salt and pepper; add to hot pan and cook 3 minutes per side, until just cooked through. Serve with green beans.

Grilled Loin Lamb Chops with Cool Cucumber Sauce

Loin lamb chops are quite small.
Some diners are satisfied with one—heartier appetites may need two.

Serves 4

Cool cucumber sauce

- 1 cup plain Greek yogurt
- 1 small cucumber, seeded and finely diced
- ⅓ cup fresh mint or parsley, chopped
- 1 scallion, thinly sliced
- Salt

Lamb chops

- ½ cup fresh mint leaves
- 2 cloves garlic, smashed
- 2 tablespoons olive oil
- 1 tablespoon balsamic vinegar
- 6 loin lamb chops

TIP: Save time by using an English cucumber, which is a seedless variety. Whichever type you use, you don't need to peel it. The green skin adds a burst of color to the sauce.

1. Preheat grill to high heat. In a small bowl, mix all sauce ingredients until combined. Refrigerate until serving.
2. In a blender, purée mint, garlic, oil and vinegar until a sauce forms. Brush mixture on both sides of chops. Grill chops about 4 minutes per side. Serve topped with cool cucumber sauce.

Garlicky Grilled Steaks

Hanger steak is a flavorful cut that's great for grilling. Before marinating, remember to remove and discard the gristle that runs down the center of the steak.

Serves 6

- 2 teaspoons fresh thyme, chopped, or 1 teaspoon dried thyme
- 1 teaspoon fresh oregano, chopped, or ½ teaspoon dried oregano
- ½ teaspoon fresh rosemary, minced, or ¼ teaspoon dried rosemary
- 6 cloves garlic, minced
- 2 pounds hanger steak
- 2 teaspoons sweet paprika
- Olive oil, for drizzling
- Salt and black pepper

TIP: Let the steak rest for 10 minutes after cooking, to allow the juices to return to the center of the meat.

1. In a mini food processor or spice grinder, combine thyme, oregano and rosemary; grind until powdery. Rub minced garlic over the steaks; sprinkle with paprika and chopped herbs. Cover with plastic and refrigerate for at least 4 hours or overnight. Let steaks stand at room temperature for 30 minutes before cooking.
2. Preheat grill or grill pan to medium-high heat. Drizzle both sides of steaks with oil; season with salt and pepper. Grill about 10 minutes per side, until charred on the outside and medium-rare on the inside, or to desired doneness. Transfer to a cutting board; let rest 10 minutes before slicing.

Flank Steak and Balsamic Spinach Salad

Pressed for time? Use a prepared balsamic vinaigrette. All you need is a crusty baguette to complete the meal.

Serves 4

Steak

1 tablespoon olive oil

1¼ pounds flank steak, cut into 4 pieces

Salt and black pepper

Salad

2 teaspoons balsamic vinegar

¼ teaspoon Dijon mustard

1 small clove garlic, minced

Salt and black pepper

2 tablespoons olive oil

4 ounces (about 4 cups) baby spinach leaves

½ pint cherry tomatoes, halved

⅓ cup walnuts, toasted and chopped

TIP: Let the pan get hot before adding the steak.

For steak:

1. Warm oil in a large cast-iron or heavy skillet over high heat. Season the steak with salt and pepper. Add to the hot pan; cook 6 minutes per side, or to desired doneness. Transfer to a cutting board; let the steak sit 5 minutes before thinly slicing it on the diagonal.

For salad:

1. Whisk vinegar, mustard, garlic, salt and pepper in a large bowl. Whisk in oil until thoroughly blended.
2. Add spinach to the bowl and, using your hands or tongs, toss gently. Mound spinach salad on 4 plates; top with the steak slices, tomatoes and a showering of walnuts.

Marinated Green and White Bean Salad with Garlic Shrimp

Sometimes the simplest recipes are the most delicious—especially when the ingredients are summer-fresh.

Serves 4

Salad

- ½ pound green beans, trimmed
- 2 tablespoons fresh lemon juice
- 2 tablespoons extra-virgin olive oil
- 1 clove garlic, minced
- ½ cup fresh Italian parsley, chopped
- 1 can (15 ounces) cannellini beans, drained
- ¼ cup Parmesan cheese, grated, plus more for garnish
- ½ pint cherry tomatoes, halved
- Salt and black pepper

Shrimp

- 2 tablespoons olive oil
- 3 cloves garlic, minced
- 12 ounces shrimp, peeled and deveined

TIP: Don't cook the beans all the way through; you just want them crisp-tender.

For salad:

1. Blanch green beans in a medium saucepan of boiling water for 2 minutes; drain and rinse in cool water. Let cool; slice in half on the diagonal.
2. In a large serving bowl, whisk lemon juice, oil and garlic until blended. Fold in parsley and cannellini beans; let the cannellini beans marinate 20 minutes while the green beans cool.

For shrimp:

1. Warm oil in a large heavy skillet over medium heat. Add garlic; cook 30 seconds, stirring. Add shrimp; cook 5 minutes, stirring often.
2. Fold cooled green beans, Parmesan and tomatoes into cannellini beans. Season with salt and pepper. Garnish with additional Parmesan. Mound shrimp atop salad.

Crunchy Pork Chops with Beet and Carrot Slaw

Mild pork chops, coated with a golden crust and served with a lime-scented slaw make a refreshing change of pace as a summer dinner.

Serves 4

Slaw

1 tablespoon fresh lime juice

1 tablespoon extra-virgin olive oil

2 tablespoons fresh Italian parsley, chopped

½ teaspoon granulated sugar

Pinch of salt

1 cup raw beets (about 1 small beet), grated and peeled

1 cup carrots (about 1 large carrot), grated

TIP: Raw beets are surprisingly sweet in this uncooked salad.

Pork chops

3 cups panko or bread crumbs

3 cloves garlic, minced

2 tablespoons vegetable or olive oil

Salt and black pepper

2 tablespoons Parmesan cheese, grated

2 tablespoons fresh Italian parsley, chopped

3 large egg whites

2 tablespoons Dijon mustard

6 tablespoons all-purpose flour

Nonstick cooking spray

4 center-cut, boneless pork chops, about 6 ounces each, 1 inch thick

Crunchy Pork Chops with Beet and Carrot Slaw

Recipe continued from previous page.

For slaw:

1. In a medium bowl, whisk lime juice, oil, parsley, sugar and salt. Fold in beets and carrots until coated. Refrigerate at least 30 minutes before serving.

For pork chops:

1. Preheat oven to 325°F. On a rimmed baking sheet, toss crumbs with garlic, oil, salt and pepper. Toss until crumbs are evenly coated with oil. Bake about 10 minutes, until golden brown, stirring twice. Transfer to a large bowl and cool to room temperature. Toss crumbs with Parmesan and parsley.
2. In a shallow bowl, whisk egg whites and mustard. Add flour and whisk until blended (there may be some clumps).
3. Preheat oven to 400°F. Spray wire rack with nonstick cooking spray and set on a rimmed baking sheet. Season chops with salt and pepper. Using tongs, dredge chops in the egg mixture; let the excess drip off. Add chops to the bread-crumb mixture, pressing gently so that crumbs adhere. Lay the breaded chops on the wire rack. Repeat with the remaining 3 chops. Bake chops 18 to 25 minutes, until an instant-read thermometer inserted into the center of the chops registers 150°F. Let the chops rest on the rack 5 minutes. Serve with slaw.

Pan-Seared Turkey Cutlets with Creamed Corn and Bacon

A creamy corn side sauté spiked with smoky bacon is a perfect partner to quick-cooking turkey breasts.

Serves 4

Creamed corn and bacon

- 3 slices bacon, chopped
- ½ small red onion, minced
- 5 ears corn, kernels scraped from cob (about 3 cups)
- ⅓ cup half-and-half or heavy cream
- 2 tablespoons chopped fresh Italian parsley
- Salt and black pepper

Turkey cutlets

- 1 tablespoon olive oil
- 4 thin (about 1 pound) turkey cutlets
- Salt, black pepper and garlic powder

TIP: Use a serrated bread knife to scrape the kernels from the cob. Place the cob in a large bowl when you cut, so the kernels don't fly everywhere.

For creamed corn and bacon:

1. In a large heavy skillet, cook bacon until crisp. Transfer to a paper towel–lined plate; crumble. Add onions to drippings in the skillet over medium-low heat. Cook 5 minutes, until softened, stirring. Add corn; cook 2 minutes, stirring often. Pour in cream and cook 2 minutes, until sauce thickens, stirring. Remove from heat; stir in bacon and parsley. Season to taste with salt and pepper.

For turkey cutlets:

1. Meanwhile, warm oil in a large heavy skillet over medium-high heat. Season turkey with salt, pepper and garlic powder. Add to hot pan; cook 3 minutes per side, until golden and cooked through. Serve with creamed corn.

CHAPTER 5

Ana Raquel had no idea what she was supposed to say to Greg's confession. Not that his feelings for her when he'd been seven had anything to do with what was happening today, but still. She stared blindly at the folders on the table.

"We, ah, should talk about the cookbook," she murmured.

"Good idea."

While he fanned out pages, she went back to the foyer to get her notebook out of her bag.

"I thought we'd divide the cookbook into seasons," she told him. "That way people can simply flip to the time of year and buy whatever is fresh and local."

Greg's expression turned smug as he passed her his notes. The first page was a division of the cookbook into seasons.

"We think alike," he told her. "Interesting. I thought we should divide each season into everyday recipes and those for special events. Like brunches or parties."

"Celebrations," she said.

"Right." He flipped through her pages. "Like this one. Birthday Party Banana Layer Cake. That's spring."

"And Celebrations," she added.

"Exactly." He studied what she'd written. "You have too many salads. I like a salad as much as the next guy—"

"Which means not at all."

He chuckled. "They have their place, but we need more substantial food. Chili or some casseroles. People in town are always bringing each other casseroles."

"And if it were a chili casserole it would be perfect?"

"You're reading my mind."

"You're such a guy," she told him. "I suppose you're also going to tell me there should be plenty of pies in the book?"

"Sure. Who doesn't love pie?"

He was less intense than she remembered. The Greg she'd known had been one determined soul. He'd run his bid to be student council president with a focus that would have left a national campaign manager envious. She'd wanted to win, too, but she also made time for her friends and her family.

"How many hours a week do you work?" she asked.

"Sixty, maybe seventy."

"No wonder there's no girlfriend. Life is more than what we make in the kitchen."

"You really believe that?" he asked, leaning back in his chair and picking up his wine.

"Sure. Mostly." She laughed. "Okay, not always, but it's important to have balance."

"I'm into balance. I'd like to have someone in my life, but finding the right girl isn't as easy as it sounds." He shrugged. "I have very specific wants."

She took in the handsome face, the long, lean body. "There have to be plenty of volunteers."

"Some."

"Many."

"I have a type."

"Which is?"

"Funny, pretty, creative." He put down his wine. "Ana Raquel, we have to talk about the elephant in the room."

Elephant? There was no elephant. He couldn't possibly mean... Only staring at his face, she knew he could and he did. "Prom?" she asked in a whisper.

"Prom night," he correctly gently.

Chapter 6 begins on page 116

sum

Picnics and Parties

Sparkling Watermelon Lemonade

Serve this pleasingly pink, super-refreshing drink at your next summer barbecue.

Makes 6 cups

Simple syrup

- ½ cup granulated sugar
- ½ cup water

Lemonade

- 8 cups seedless watermelon cubes
- 4 lemons, juiced, enough to equal 1 cup of lemon juice
- Sparkling water or seltzer
- Fresh mint leaves, for garnish

TIP: Simple syrup is a great sweetener to have on hand for blending drinks.

For simple syrup:

1. In a small pan over medium-high heat, combine sugar and ½ cup water. Cook 5 minutes, until sugar is dissolved. Pour into a liquid measuring cup and let cool.

For lemonade:

1. In a blender or food processor, pulse the watermelon until smooth. Strain puréed watermelon to remove seeds and pulp. Return watermelon liquid to the blender. Add lemon juice and ½ cup simple syrup; pulse until blended. Chill until serving. Serve over ice, with a splash of sparkling water and fresh mint as a garnish.

Zucchini Ricotta Toasts

A quick sauté with a bit of garlic paired with a dollop of ricotta cheese makes a savory topping for this delicious summer appetizer.

Toasts

- ¼ cup olive oil
- 1 large clove garlic, smashed
- 1 small baguette

Topping

- 1 tablespoon olive oil
- 1 medium zucchini, trimmed and diced
- 1 clove garlic, minced
- Salt and black pepper
- 1 cup ricotta cheese
- 2 tablespoons fresh herbs (tarragon, mint, dill or chives), chopped

TIP: Make the toasts up to 2 days in advance. Store, tightly covered, at room temperature.

For toasts:

1. Pour olive oil into a small cup; add smashed garlic clove and let the garlic and oil sit for 5 minutes. Preheat oven to 300°F. Cut baguette into twenty ¼-inch diagonal slices; place them on a baking sheet. Brush with garlic oil. Bake 10 to 15 minutes, until lightly golden and crisp.

For topping:

1. Warm oil in a large nonstick skillet over medium heat. Add zucchini; cook 8 minutes, until softened and golden, stirring often. Add garlic; cook 30 seconds, stirring. Season to taste with salt and pepper.
2. In a small bowl, combine ricotta, herbs, salt and pepper. Evenly spread ricotta over cooled toasts. Top with zucchini mixture.

Tiny Parmesan Biscuits with Caramelized Onions and Crème Fraiche

Cooking onions for a long time over low heat brings out their sweetness.

Makes 18–20

Biscuits

- ⅓ cup all-purpose flour
- ¼ teaspoon salt
- 3 tablespoons cold unsalted butter, chopped
- ⅔ cup Parmesan cheese, grated

Topping

- 2 teaspoons olive oil
- 1 medium onion, very thinly sliced
- 1 teaspoon granulated sugar
- Salt and black pepper
- ½ cup crème fraiche
- 2 tablespoons chopped fresh chives

TIP: Crème fraiche is a thickened cream, similar to sour cream, with a less sour, more buttery flavor.

For biscuits:

1. Line a baking sheet with parchment paper or a nonstick baking pad. In a food processor, pulse flour, salt, butter and cheese just until dough holds together when pinched with your fingers. Scrape dough onto a lightly floured surface; roll to ¼-inch thickness. Using a 1½-inch fluted cookie cutter, cut out as many rounds as possible. Place rounds on the prepared sheet 1 inch apart. Refrigerate 20 minutes.
2. Preheat oven to 350°F. Bake biscuits 8 minutes, until lightly browned throughout. Transfer to a wire rack to cool.

For topping:

1. Warm oil in a large nonstick skillet over medium heat. When pan is hot, add onions, sugar, salt and pepper. Reduce heat to low; cook 30 minutes, until deep golden brown and caramelized, stirring often.
2. Top each biscuit with 1 teaspoon each of crème fraiche and onions. Garnish with chives.

Broccoli, Cheddar and Bacon Quiche

In this classic brunch dish, broccoli gives the silky egg-and-cheese filling a nice crunch. If the crust is filled to the top, bake the quiche tin on a baking sheet to catch any spills.

Serves 4

Crust

- 1½ cups cheddar cheese, grated, and divided
- 1 prepared pie crust (about 9 inches)

Filling

- 5 slices bacon
- 1 small shallot, minced
- 1 small stalk broccoli, florets diced (about 1½ cups)
- ¼ cup water
- 2 large eggs
- 1 cup whole milk
- 1 teaspoon salt

TIP: Quiche will keep, refrigerated, tightly covered, up to 3 days. To reheat, cover with foil and warm in a 325°F oven for about 15 minutes.

For crust:

1. Preheat oven to 350°F. Sprinkle ½ cup of the cheese over the bottom of the pie crust.

For filling:

1. Cook the bacon in a heavy medium skillet until crisp. Transfer to a paper towel–lined plate to drain; crumble. Drain off most of the fat from the skillet. Add shallots; cook about 1 minute, until softened, stirring. Add chopped broccoli and ¼ cup water; cook 5 minutes, stirring. Stir in crumbled bacon.
2. In a large bowl, whisk eggs, milk and salt until frothy. Spoon the broccoli-shallot mixture over the cheese in the pie tin. Pour the custard over the vegetables. Sprinkle the remaining cheese on top.
3. Bake for 30 minutes, until the edges are set but the quiche still jiggles a little in the center. Cool for at least 20 minutes, or overnight.

Eggplant Parmesan Pizza

Pizza is so much more delicious when you bake it yourself. And super-easy when you start with a prepared pizza crust.

Serves 4

- Oil and cornmeal, for pan
- 1 clove garlic, smashed
- 4 tablespoons olive oil
- 1 medium eggplant, trimmed and cut into ¼-inch slices
- Salt and black pepper
- 1 cup ricotta cheese
- 1 cup Parmesan cheese, grated, and divided
- 1 pound prepared pizza dough
- ½ cup marinara sauce
- 1 cup mozzarella cheese, shredded
- Fresh basil, thinly sliced

TIP: You may need more oil as the eggplant cooks.

1. Preheat oven to 425°F. Lightly oil a large baking sheet; sprinkle with cornmeal.
2. Preheat grill or grill pan over high heat. In a small cup, combine smashed garlic and oil. Brush eggplant with the garlic oil; grill 4 minutes per side, until soft and golden. Season with salt and pepper.
3. In a small bowl, whisk ricotta and ¼ cup of the Parmesan until combined.
4. Roll out pizza dough on a lightly floured surface to a 9-by-13-inch rectangle. Transfer to the prepared sheet. Spread marinara sauce over the dough. Drop ricotta mixture over the sauce. Lay eggplant slices over the ricotta; sprinkle with mozzarella and the remaining Parmesan. Bake 16 to 18 minutes, until crust is crisp and the bottom of the pizza is lightly browned. Sprinkle basil over pizza. Let the pizza sit 5 minutes before slicing.

Life-Changing Guacamole

Guacamole is always the first thing to go at a party—
especially when it's homemade.

Makes 2 cups

- 2 ripe avocados, diced
- 2 tablespoons red onion, minced
- 1 clove garlic, minced
- 2 tablespoons fresh lime juice, or as needed
- 1 tablespoon extra-virgin olive oil
- 2 tablespoons fresh cilantro, minced
- ½ small tomato, diced
- ½ fresh jalapeño pepper, seeded and finely chopped
- Salt

TIP: Remember to make the dip as close to serving time as possible.

1. In a medium serving bowl, combine avocados, onions, garlic, lime juice and oil. Using a fork or potato masher, mash until the mixture turns into a thick purée. Stir in cilantro, tomatoes and jalapeños. Season to taste with salt and additional lime juice, if desired.

Roasted Potato Salad

No summer picnic is complete without potato salad.
This one is deliciously different because the potatoes are roasted.

Serves 8

Nonstick cooking spray
6 baking potatoes, peeled and cut into ¾-inch chunks
2 tablespoons olive oil
Salt and black pepper
1½ cups mayonnaise
1 tablespoon Dijon mustard
½ teaspoon celery seed, optional
4 hard-boiled eggs, peeled and diced
2 scallions, thinly sliced
2 stalks celery, thinly sliced
1 kosher pickle, diced
¼ cup fresh Italian parsley, chopped
Paprika, for garnish

TIP: Feel free to use reduced-fat or light mayonnaise.

1. Preheat oven to 400°F. Coat two baking sheets with nonstick cooking spray. In a large bowl, toss chopped potato with oil, salt and pepper. Spread potatoes in a single layer onto the prepared sheets. Bake 30 minutes, until lightly golden and tender, but still with some bite. Remove the baking sheets from the oven and allow potatoes to cool slightly.
2. In a medium bowl, whisk mayonnaise and mustard until combined. Add cooled potatoes, celery seed (if desired), eggs, scallions, celery, pickle and parsley. Fold mixture to coat with mayonnaise and combine flavors. Season to taste with salt and pepper. Garnish with paprika.

Black Bean and Corn Confetti Salad

Serve this August classic either as a salad or as a hearty dip with chops.

Serves 4

- ¼ cup extra-virgin olive oil
- 3 tablespoons fresh lime juice
- 1 tablespoon ground cumin
- 1 clove garlic, minced
- Dash hot pepper sauce
- Salt and black pepper
- 3 ears corn
- 1 can (15 ounces) black beans, drained and rinsed
- 1 can (4½ ounces) minced green chilies, if desired
- 4 ounces Monterey Jack cheese, cut into small chunks
- 1 small red onion, finely chopped
- ¼ cup fresh cilantro, chopped

TIP: When corn is fresh, there's no need to cook it for a salad.

1. In a large serving bowl, whisk oil, lime juice, cumin, garlic, pepper sauce, salt and pepper until combined.
2. Using a serrated knife, scrape kernels off ears of corn. Add to bowl. Add remaining ingredients; toss until combined. Add more lime juice, cumin, salt and pepper as desired.

Tomato Salad with Molasses Vinaigrette

A simple plate of tomatoes becomes much more interesting when drizzled with a sweet-tart molasses vinaigrette.

- 2 tablespoons extra-virgin olive oil
- 2 tablespoons red-wine vinegar
- 1½ teaspoons molasses
- 1 clove garlic, minced
- Salt and black pepper
- 2 large tomatoes, cut into thin wedges
- ½ cup red or sweet onion, very thinly sliced
- ¼ cup sliced fresh basil

TIP: Show off the vibrant tomatoes of the season by serving this salad on a bright blue plate.

1. In a medium serving bowl, whisk oil, vinegar, molasses, garlic, salt and pepper until blended. Add remaining ingredients; toss lightly to coat. Allow to marinate for at least 30 minutes before serving.

BBQ Chicken Salad

All the flavors your family loves in one big main-dish salad. Go ahead and make it year-round.

Serves 6

Dressing

- ¼ cup prepared ranch dressing
- ¼ cup prepared BBQ sauce
- ¼ cup fresh cilantro, chopped, plus additional for garnish
- 1 tablespoon fresh lime juice

Salad

- 4 boneless, skinless chicken breast halves
- 1 large head romaine lettuce, chopped
- 1 cup canned black beans, drained
- 1 large avocado, diced
- 1 cup cherry tomatoes, quartered
- ½ small red onion, diced
- 1 cup Monterey Jack cheese, shredded or cubed
- Crushed tortilla chips, for garnish

TIP: Recipe doubles easily to serve a crowd.

For dressing:

1. In a small bowl, whisk all ingredients together until blended.

For salad:

1. Grill chicken until it reaches desired doneness. Let it cool slightly; thinly slice on the diagonal.
2. On a large platter, gently toss lettuce, beans, avocados, tomatoes, onions and cheese. Toss with about half of the dressing. Top salad with chicken; drizzle with remaining dressing. Garnish with chips.

Spinach and Nectarine Salad with Pecans and Warm Bacon Vinaigrette

Tired of the same old tossed green salad?
Wake up your taste buds with this fun flavor combination.

- 6 slices bacon
- 2 tablespoons shallots, chopped
- 2 tablespoons white-wine vinegar
- ½ teaspoon Dijon mustard
- Salt and black pepper
- 2 ripe nectarines
- 6 ounces baby spinach
- ½ cup chopped toasted pecans

TIP: Make this salad in summertime, when nectarines are ripest.

1. In a large heavy skillet, cook bacon until crisp. Transfer to a paper towel–lined plate; crumble. Drain off 3 tablespoons of the drippings into a small bowl. Add shallots, vinegar, mustard, salt and pepper; whisk until blended. (Discard remaining drippings.)
2. Over a large serving bowl, cut nectarines into 1-inch chunks. Spoon out about 1 tablespoon of juice released from slicing; whisk into bacon dressing. In the same large bowl, toss nectarines (and any remaining juice) with spinach and pecans. Pour dressing over salad. Add bacon; toss to combine.

Grilled Steak Caesar Salad

It's fun to make your own Caesar dressing for special occasions. If you're pressed for time, reach for your favorite bottled brand.

Serves 6

Steak

- ½ cup mayonnaise
- 2 tablespoons fresh lemon juice
- 2 teaspoons Dijon mustard
- 2 oil-packed anchovies, drained
- 1 large clove garlic
- ½ teaspoon Worcestershire sauce
- Dash Tabasco sauce
- ⅓ cup Parmesan cheese, grated, plus additional for garnish
- 4 tablespoons olive oil, divided
- Salt and black pepper
- One 2-pound flank steak

Croutons

- 1 small baguette, cut into 1-inch cubes

Salad

- 1 pound romaine hearts, cut into 1-inch strips
- 1 large bunch watercress
- 2 large heirloom or beefsteak tomatoes, very thinly sliced

TIP: To prep watercress, give stalks a quick rinse, then slice off the woody ends of the stems. Cut the remaining stalks in half to use in salad.

For steak:

1. Preheat oven to 375°F. In a food processor, pulse mayonnaise, lemon juice, mustard, anchovies, garlic, Worcestershire, Tabasco, Parmesan, 3 tablespoons of the oil, salt and pepper until smooth. In a plastic container, spread ¼ cup of the dressing over the steak; refrigerate for at least 30 minutes.

For croutons:

1. On a rimmed baking sheet, toss baguette cubes with the remaining 1 tablespoon oil; season with salt and pepper. Bake 10 minutes, until golden, turning croutons occasionally. Let cool.

To cook steak:

1. Preheat grill to medium-high heat. Season the steak with salt and pepper. Grill steak to desired doneness. Transfer steak to a cutting board and let it rest for 5 minutes.

For salad:

1. In a large bowl, toss romaine, watercress, tomatoes, croutons and reserved dressing. Thinly slice the steak across the grain on the diagonal. Mound salad on serving plates; top with the steak slices.

Henri's Ratatouille with Shaved Parmesan

Although traditionally served as a side dish, ratatouille also makes a fantastic pasta sauce, sandwich condiment or pizza topping.

- ¼ cup olive oil
- 1 large eggplant, chopped into ¾-inch dice
- Salt and black pepper
- 2 medium zucchini, chopped into ½-inch dice
- 2 teaspoons fresh thyme leaves, chopped
- 1 small onion, chopped
- 2 large tomatoes, chopped, juices saved
- 2 tablespoons prepared pesto, plus more if desired
- 2 teaspoons red-wine vinegar
- ¾ cup Parmesan shavings

TIP: For a striking visual accent, use a vegetable peeler to make the Parmesan shavings.

1. Warm oil in a large heavy skillet over medium-low heat. Add eggplant; season with salt and pepper. Cook 10 minutes, until soft, stirring often to prevent sticking. Add zucchini and thyme; cook 10 minutes, stirring to coat zucchini with oil from eggplant. Add onions; cook 4 minutes, stirring. Add tomatoes; cook 8 minutes, until tomatoes break down and release their liquid. Mixture will become slightly saucy.
2. Remove from heat; stir in pesto and vinegar. Serve warm or at room temperature. Sprinkle with cheese before serving.

Raspberry Crumble Cake

Although this cake is sweet enough for dessert, it also makes a sensational breakfast.

Serves 10

Cake

- Butter, to grease pan
- 2 cups all-purpose flour, plus additional for pan
- 1 teaspoon baking soda
- 1 teaspoon baking powder
- ½ teaspoon salt
- 1 teaspoon ground cinnamon
- ½ cup (1 stick) unsalted butter, at room temperature
- 1 cup granulated sugar
- 2 large eggs, at room temperature
- 2 teaspoons pure vanilla extract
- 1 cup sour cream or plain, full-fat Greek yogurt
- 2 cups fresh raspberries (or thawed frozen)

Topping

- ½ cup all-purpose flour
- ¼ cup light-brown sugar
- ½ cup walnuts, chopped
- 3 tablespoons unsalted butter, melted

For cake:

1. Preheat oven to 350°F. Lightly grease and flour the top and sides of a 9-inch cake pan with removable bottom. In a medium bowl, whisk flour, baking soda, baking powder, salt and cinnamon until combined.
2. In a large bowl with an electric mixer on high speed, beat butter until creamy. Add sugar; beat until light and fluffy. Add eggs and vanilla; beat until blended. Alternately add dry ingredients and sour cream, beating just until combined.
3. Spoon half of the mixture into the prepared pan. Evenly sprinkle berries on top of batter. Top with remaining batter.

For topping:

1. In a small bowl, whisk flour, brown sugar and nuts. Add butter; mix with fingers until dough forms pea-sized clumps. Sprinkle topping evenly over fruit. Bake 60 to 65 minutes, until a toothpick inserted in the center comes out clean. Transfer to a wire rack to cool.

TIP: If you're using Greek yogurt, stick to full-fat varieties for baking.

Ambrosia Bakery's Chocolate Mocha Cupcakes

You can't go wrong with rich chocolate cupcakes topped with a luscious swirl of mocha frosting.

Makes 14

Cupcakes

- 1½ cups (3 sticks) unsalted butter, chopped
- 7 ounces semisweet chocolate, chips or chopped
- 1 tablespoon instant espresso powder
- 4 large eggs
- 1 cup granulated sugar
- 1⅔ cups all-purpose flour
- Pinch of salt

Frosting

- 3 ounces semisweet chocolate, chips or chopped
- 1 teaspoon instant espresso powder
- 12 tablespoons (1½ sticks) unsalted butter
- 2 teaspoons pure vanilla extract
- 3 cups sifted powdered sugar
- 3–5 tablespoons heavy cream, as needed

For cupcakes:

1. Preheat oven to 325°F. Line 14 muffin cups with paper liners.
2. Melt butter and chocolate in microwave; stir in espresso powder to dissolve. In a large bowl with an electric mixer on high speed, beat eggs and sugar for 5 minutes, until light and thick. Add chocolate mixture to blend. Remove from mixer; fold in flour and salt just until blended.
3. Spoon batter into muffin cups. Bake 20 to 24 minutes, until just firm to the touch. Cool in pans for 5 minutes; remove to wire racks to cool completely.

For frosting:

1. Melt chocolate in microwave; stir espresso powder into hot chocolate to dissolve. Cream butter in a large bowl with an electric mixer on high speed. Add vanilla; beat until blended. Add ¼ cup of the powdered sugar; beat until blended. Add melted chocolate mixture; beat until blended. Alternately mix in remaining powdered sugar and cream, beating after each addition and using only as much cream as necessary to reach desired consistency.
2. Fit a pastry bag with a large star tip. Fill bag with frosting. Using a circular motion, pipe a swirl of frosting on each cooled cupcake.

TIP: Wait until the cupcakes are completely cool before frosting them.

S'mores Bars

No campfire required
for these kid-friendly treats.

- 6 tablespoons unsalted butter, plus additional for greasing the pan
- 1½ cups graham cracker crumbs (from about 10 whole crackers)
- ¾ cup sweetened condensed milk
- 1¼ cups semisweet chocolate chips
- Pinch of salt
- 1¼ cups mini-marshmallows
- 1 whole graham cracker, broken into bits

TIP: Note—you won't use the whole can of condensed milk. Use leftover milk as a sweet addition to hot or iced coffee.

1. Butter the bottom and sides of an 8-inch-square baking dish.
2. Melt butter in a medium bowl in the microwave. Add graham cracker crumbs and stir until evenly moistened and mixture holds together. Press mixture evenly into the bottom of prepared pan.
3. Combine condensed milk and chocolate chips in a medium saucepan; place over medium-low heat. Warm until chocolate is melted and smooth, stirring often. Remove from heat; stir in salt. Pour over graham cracker base, smoothing with a spatula. Drop marshmallows over the warm chocolate, gently pressing so marshmallows become embedded in the chocolate. Break up the whole graham cracker and stick the pieces in between the marshmallows. Cover the pan and refrigerate at least 3 hours. Serve cold.

Henri's Tarte Tatin

A fancy French-style tart that just looks hard to make.
It's best served warm with vanilla ice cream.

Serves 8

- 6 medium tart apples, such as Golden Delicious, peeled, cored and quartered
- 1¼ cups granulated sugar, divided
- 6 tablespoons unsalted butter, cut into 6 chunks
- 1 sheet puff pastry, defrosted if frozen

TIP: The apple wedges will seem too big at first, but will cook down in the bubbling caramel.

1. In a large bowl, toss apple chunks with ¼ cup of the sugar. Let sit 10 minutes to release juices.
2. Melt butter in a 10-inch cast-iron or heavy ovenproof skillet over medium-low heat. Using a pastry brush, brush melted butter along the edges of the skillet to grease the sides. Stir in remaining 1 cup sugar. Cook until sugar is dissolved and lightly golden. Remove pan from heat; lay apples on top of the sugar in concentric circles. Push and squeeze the apples so that they all fit in pan—it's all right if they rest on top of each other. Return pan to stove, still over medium-low heat. Cook 20 to 25 minutes, without stirring, until apples are softened. Press down on the apples as they cook to baste them in the caramel.
3. Preheat oven to 375°F. On a lightly floured surface, roll out the pastry to a 10-inch circle. Lay the pastry round over the apples; tuck in the edges of the pastry. Slice 4 vents in the pastry. Transfer to the oven; bake 20 minutes, until top is browned. Transfer to a wire rack and cool at least 10 minutes.
4. Run spatula around the edges of the skillet. Invert a cake plate over the skillet and, using pot holders to hold the skillet and plate tightly together, invert tart onto the plate. If any apples remain in the skillet, scrape them off and fit them into the tart. Scrape any excess caramel from the skillet and add to the tart.

Fun Apple Fritters with Caramel Dipping Sauce

Fritters are best served hot.
So gather the family in the kitchen and have a fritter fest!

Fritters

- 2 apples, such Golden Delicious, peeled, cored and chopped into large chunks
- ¼ cup light-brown sugar
- 2 tablespoons granulated sugar
- 1 teaspoon ground cinnamon
- 1 cup all-purpose flour
- Pinch of salt
- 8 ounces sparkling apple cider
- Peanut or vegetable oil, for frying

Caramel sauce

- 6 ounces caramel candies, unwrapped
- 2 tablespoons milk or heavy cream

TIP: Don't worry about the shape of the fritters. The craggy sides are part of their charm.

For fritters:

1. In a bowl, toss apples, both sugars and cinnamon. In a large bowl, whisk flour and salt. Make a well in the center of the dry ingredients and pour in the cider; whisk until blended. Fold in the apple mixture until coated. Let the batter rest 10 minutes.
2. In a medium-deep pot, add oil to a depth of at least 2 inches. Heat oil to a temperature of 360°F. Using a large tablespoon, scoop up a heaping spoonful of the apple mixture and gently drop it into the oil. Fry about 4 minutes, until golden brown on all sides, flipping once. You should be able to fry about 3 fritters in each batch. Using a slotted spoon, remove the cooked fritters to a paper towel–lined platter.

For caramel sauce:

1. Bring a pot of water to a simmer over high heat. Place a metal bowl on top of the simmering water. Place caramels and milk in the bowl; reduce heat to low. Melt caramels, stirring constantly. Pour into a serving bowl. Serve with hot fritters.

Denise's Summer Berry Pie

Double crust

- 2½ cups all-purpose flour, plus additional for rolling
- 1 tablespoon granulated sugar, plus additional for baking
- ¼ teaspoon salt
- 1 cup (2 sticks) unsalted butter, cold and cut into cubes
- ¼–½ cup cold water

Filling

- 6½ cups blueberries, blackberries and/or raspberries
- ½ cup granulated sugar
- ¼ cup light-brown sugar
- 2 tablespoons fresh lemon juice
- Pinch of salt
- ¼ cup instant tapioca or cornstarch

TIP: Adding a bit of tapioca to fruit pies helps prevent the filling from becoming too runny.

For crust:

1. In food processor, pulse flour, sugar and salt until combined. Add butter; pulse until the mixture resembles coarse meal. Slowly add cold water, a little at a time, just until dough comes together into a craggy mass. Turn the dough out onto a floured surface; roughly knead dough until it holds together. Divide the dough in half. Form each half into a thick disk; wrap in plastic and refrigerate at least 1 hour or up to 2 days.
2. Remove dough from refrigerator about 20 minutes before rolling out. Generously flour surface. Using a floured rolling pin, roll out the first disk to a 12-inch circle. Transfer to a glass pie tin. Press dough to fit the tin; flute the edges. Refrigerate at least 30 minutes.

The polka-dot crust of this berry pie makes it a show-stopping party dessert.
It's also more forgiving than a lattice crust.

For filling:

1. In a large bowl, combine berries, both sugars, lemon juice and salt. Let sit at room temperature for 30 minutes. Stir in tapioca until mostly dissolved.
2. Preheat oven to 425°F. Remove crust from refrigerator. Line pie crust with parchment and fill with pie weights or beans. Bake 20 minutes; remove from oven and lift off parchment. Bake another 10 to 15 minutes until just starting to brown. Transfer to a wire rack; let cool slightly. Reduce oven temperature to 350°F.
3. While the crust bakes, roll out the remaining dough on a floured surface to a 10-inch circle. Using several round cookie or biscuit cutters in different sizes, cut out as many circles as possible. Lay the circles of dough on a wire rack; refrigerate while the crust bakes and cools.
4. Pour filling into crust. Top the filling with the circles of dough, overlapping them to fill the top of the pie. Sprinkle with granulated sugar. Bake 1 hour, until crust is browned and fruit bubbles. Transfer to a wire rack to cool. Let the pie cool at least 2 hours.

CHAPTER 6

Ana Raquel's warm, relaxed feeling faded as heat burned on her cheeks. Was he kidding? There was no way she wanted to talk about that night. She'd been so determined to tell him exactly what she thought of him, only to end up giving him her virginity in a hotel room. Worse, she'd realized that she might have feelings for the one guy who'd made her totally crazy. And not in a good way. That wasn't the sort of thing she was likely to reminisce fondly about.

"You okay?" he asked.

"Fine."

"You seem upset."

"I'm not." At least she wouldn't be when they stopped talking about that night. Because she couldn't explain what had happened. One second she'd been yelling and then they'd been kissing and then...

The thing was, she wasn't that kind of girl. She'd never been serious about a boy in high school. There had been too many other things to do. Besides, being annoyed with Greg had taken all her emotional energy.

Since then, no one had really captured her attention. After having lost her virginity so foolishly, she was determined to be more careful the next time.

No doubt he was happy to jump from bed to bed. It wasn't as if she'd been his first. If she had been, he wouldn't have been able to figure out how inexperienced she was. Yet another humiliating moment he had to answer for.

"Ana Raquel? We have to talk about it. I tried to talk to you afterwards, but you'd left town. I wanted to make sure you were okay."

He was going to keep talking, she thought frantically. Talking and talking and she couldn't stand that. There was no way she was going to talk about that night. Not now, not ever. Her choices seemed to be either figuring out how to shut him up or bolting. And since they still had a cookbook to organize, she decided to shut him up.

She made sure she wasn't in danger of knocking over her wine, then reached for the front of Greg's shirt. She grabbed the soft fabric with both hands, pulled him to her and pressed her mouth to his.

They'd kissed before, she thought hazily, feeling the warmth of his mouth on hers and the way his arms came around her. But that had been different. More frantic.

This kiss was soft. He had an air of patience about him. As if they had all the time in the world. His strong arms drew her close. They were sitting in chairs, so there was no way for that to happen. Still, the pressure was insistent, so she unexpectedly found herself standing.

He rose as well, which meant he was now a lot taller than she was. She had to tilt her head back and then raise herself up on her tiptoes. But it was worth it. Because kissing Greg was like tasting the first maple syrup of the season. Sweet and filled with promise.

It was a good kiss, she thought, her eyes fluttering closed. The kind of kiss that changed a woman's perspective about nearly everything. It was a kiss that could make her want to dream about possibilities. About—

No, she thought, pulling back in a panic. This was Greg Clary, her nemesis. She might not hate him, but she really, really disliked him. They couldn't kiss. This was a kiss-free project.

She stared at him for a second. He opened his mouth to speak, but whatever he was going to say, she didn't want to hear. She bolted from the room, raced to the foyer where she grabbed her coat and her bag and then she was gone.

Chapter 7 begins on page 119

CHAPTER 7

Despite the shorter days and cooler temperatures, Ana Raquel was still busy through lunch in her trailer. She'd found a spot that attracted good foot traffic, and didn't offend any of the already established restaurants in town. As she scooped out another serving of Mushroom and Three-Cheese Lasagna, she wondered what she was going to do with herself when the weather got really cold. No one was going to dash out to eat at a street cart when it was close to freezing and damp.

She had already made arrangements to store the trailer, but she was more worried about herself. Should she look for a job in town? Leave and head south? Backpack through Europe? While backpacking across the continent sounded like fun, she didn't have the money. Besides, she had a cookbook to work on. Which meant that getting a job locally was her best option.

Without wanting to, she remembered her brief evening with Greg two nights before. They were supposed to have talked about the cookbook. Unfortunately, fate in the form of a yummy kiss had intervened. She still wasn't sure what to do about that. Should she talk about what had happened or simply pretend everything was normal between them?

"This is probably stupid."

Exactly what she was thinking, Ana Raquel thought, only she hadn't spoken. She glanced at her next customer, then smiled when she recognized Dakota Hendrix—one of the Hendrix triplets. Only she was Dakota Andersson now. Like all her sisters, she'd married and started a family. The circle of life, Ana Raquel thought wistfully. She wanted to be in a circle, too.

Dakota held out the sheet of paper in her hand.

"What is stupid?" Ana Raquel asked. "Because if you're thinking you want to save room for a muffin with your lunch, you're right. I have two choices today and they're both great."

Dakota, a pretty blond with a toddler on her hip, laughed. "I meant this."

She held out the paper. Ana Raquel took it and studied the recipe. It was for roast chicken and mashed potatoes. A seemingly simple dish made delicious with a few key ingredients.

"I heard about the cookbook," Dakota told her. "That you wanted people to volunteer recipes. This isn't that fancy..."

"Stop!" Ana Raquel shook the paper. "This is exactly what I'm looking for. Thank you."

Dakota ordered lunch, then took her food and stepped away.

Ana Raquel glanced at her watch. It was nearly time for her to close. She was going to miss her customers, she thought as she turned back to start cleaning up her kitchen.

"Any chimichangas left?"

She looked up and saw Greg standing at the open door of her trailer. The sun was behind him, putting him in silhouette. The second she recognized him, her heart began a strange kind of two-step. Part anticipation, part need to sputter and apologize. Because the last time she'd seen Greg, they'd been kissing. Well, technically she'd been running but only after the kissing.

She forced herself to pretend a calm she didn't feel as she put the last chimichanga on a plate.

He took it and settled at the small table in the trailer. As if he belonged there.

"We never did get a schedule together for working on the cookbook," he said as he unwrapped a plastic fork. "We'll need several meetings to cull the recipes, then some time in the kitchen to try each one. I'm thinking we'll need around 150 in total. What do you think?"

She thought he was amazingly cool and collected, considering the whole kissing thing. He was sitting there, eating, as if their lips had never touched.

"A hundred and fifty sounds right," she said at last, because she wasn't going to bring up the you-know-what.

"I'm working most nights at the restaurant," he said, when he'd chewed and swallowed. "Delicious, by the way." He pointed his fork at the chimichanga. "Just the right spices. We should put this in the book."

"Thanks. Sure. I have a list of street food I thought would be good." She cautiously sat across from him. "I'm going to be closing down the trailer in the next couple of weeks. Once that happens, we can start testing the recipes. If we have our list of maybes together by then, we can be ready to start cooking."

He looked at her and smiled. "Sounds like a plan. Want to use my kitchen?"

She was nervous about going back to his house, but her kitchen was the size of a shoebox and while the trailer kitchen was pretty sweet, it wasn't exactly built for two.

"Sure."

"What time are you done here?" he asked.

"About two or two-thirty."

"Do you mind coming by the restaurant after that? I can start my prep work early so we have an hour or so to go through the recipes."

She nodded. "I've heard good things about your place," she admitted. "People really like the food."

"I'm enjoying the work and being creative. But it's a lot of work. More than I expected." His expression turned rueful. "My uncle warned me that being my own boss was harder than I thought. He was right." His gaze turned intense. "What are you going to do when you shut down the trailer for the season? I could use someone like you at the restaurant."

Work for Greg? Could she? Did she want to? She had no idea if their styles would be similar. Besides, this was Greg. They weren't friends. They were...

She realized she no longer thought of him as someone she had to best. That in the years since she'd last seen him, he'd become a great guy. Or maybe he'd always been great but she'd been too busy—

With a monstrous crash, something collided with the entire trailer, which shuddered with a distinct lean to the left. The walls shook and Ana Raquel was nearly thrown from her seat. Greg was out of his chair and pulling her close before she'd even caught her breath. Outside, someone screamed.

Chapter 8 begins on page 150

Breakfast and Brunch

Triple Berry Cooler

No sugary shake, this cool drink provides a powerful blend of sweet berries and creamy yogurt. Feel free to experiment with different yogurt flavors.

- 1 small banana, frozen and cut into large chunks
- ¾ cup fresh or frozen raspberries
- ¾ cup fresh or frozen blueberries
- ¾ cup (6 ounces) strawberry-flavored nonfat yogurt
- ¼ cup skim milk, or as needed
- Crushed ice or small ice cubes, as needed

TIP: Make this super-icy by freezing berries for 10 minutes before using. (Or use frozen berries.)

1. In a blender or food processor, process banana chunks and berries to tiny bits. Add remaining ingredients; process until smooth. Add more milk or ice until you reach the desired consistency. Pour into tall glasses; garnish with additional berries, if desired.

Tropical Smoothie

For the best flavor, use the ripest mango you can find. If they aren't in season, substitute frozen mango chunks (no need to thaw).

- 1 ripe mango, peeled and cut into chunks (or 1½ cups frozen chunks)
- 1 ripe banana, cut into chunks and frozen
- ½ cup orange juice
- 6 ounces vanilla or pineapple nonfat Greek yogurt
- 1–2 cups ice chips
- Shredded coconut, optional, for garnish

TIP: Greek yogurt is thicker and has a richer flavor than regular yogurt. Either can be used in this recipe.

1. In a blender or food processor, process mango and banana chunks with orange juice until blended. Add remaining ingredients; process until smooth. Add ice to desired consistency. Pour into tall glasses; garnish with coconut, if desired.

California Harvest Granola

This crunchy, crispy cereal stars some homegrown California produce.
It makes a big batch, but will keep for at least a week in an airtight container.

Makes 8 cups

- 3 cups old-fashioned oats (not quick-cooking)
- 1 cup oat bran
- 1 cup whole almonds, coarsely chopped
- ½ cup sunflower seeds
- ⅓ cup light-brown sugar
- 1 teaspoon salt
- ½ teaspoon ground cinnamon
- ½ cup coconut oil
- 2 large egg whites (or ¼ cup whites)
- ½ pound dates, pitted and coarsely chopped

TIPS: Warming the liquid, although not required, helps it to coat the grains. If you can't find coconut oil, use maple syrup.

1. Preheat oven to 325°F. Line 2 large-rimmed baking sheets with parchment paper.
2. In a large bowl, combine oats, oat bran, almonds, seeds, brown sugar, salt and cinnamon. In a microwave, warm oil and egg whites 20 seconds, until oil is slightly liquefied. Stir liquid into dry ingredients until grains are well coated. Spread mixture evenly onto prepared sheets. Bake 20 minutes. Remove sheets from the oven; stir mixture so outer grains don't become overtoasted. Rotate baking sheets; return them to the oven for 10 more minutes, until mixture is lightly golden and evenly toasted. Transfer sheets to wire racks; let mixture completely cool on racks. Pour into a large bowl; toss with chopped dates. Store in a tightly covered container.

Everything Bagel Crisps

Got some day-old bagels? Make bagel crisps for your next brunch.
Crisps can be made in advance, and stored in an airtight container for up to 2 weeks.

3 tablespoons olive oil

1 large clove garlic, crushed

1 everything bagel

4 ounces cream cheese, at room temperature

1 tablespoon fresh lemon juice

1 teaspoon lemon zest, grated

4 ounces smoked salmon, cut into 24 strips

Garnishes

24 small dill sprigs

Capers

TIP: Smoked salmon may be expensive, but you only need a small strip on each crisp.

1. Preheat oven to 300°F. Line a baking sheet with parchment paper or a nonstick baking pad. Combine oil and crushed garlic in a small bowl; let steep for 5 minutes.
2. Using a serrated bread knife, carefully cut the bagel vertically into quarters. Turn each quarter cut-side down and slice horizontally into 6 thin wedges. You should now have 24 thin wedges. Arrange wedges on the prepared baking sheet. Using a pastry brush, lightly coat one side of each wedge with the garlic oil. Bake 16 minutes, until golden and crisp. Transfer to wire rack to cool.
3. In a small bowl, stir cream cheese, lemon juice and zest until blended. Top each cooled crisp with about 1 teaspoon cream cheese mixture. Roll up salmon strips and nestle into cream cheese mixture. Garnish with a small dill sprig and a couple of capers.

Strawberries and Cream Kringle

Kringle is a type of sweet, filled Danish—often formed in a pretzel or oval shape. This version is super-easy, thanks to a prepared puff pastry.

Serves 6

Filling

- 4 ounces cream cheese, at room temperature
- ½ cup powdered sugar
- ¼ teaspoon almond extract

Pastry

- 1 sheet frozen puff pastry, thawed
- ¾ cup strawberry or raspberry jam

Icing

- ¾ cup powdered sugar
- ½ teaspoon pure vanilla extract
- 3 teaspoons whole milk, as needed

TIP: Using cream cheese at room temperature makes the blending easier.

For filling:

1. Preheat oven to 375°F. Line a baking sheet with parchment paper or nonstick liner. In a medium bowl, beat cream cheese, powdered sugar and almond extract until blended.

For pastry:

1. On a lightly floured surface, roll pastry to a 9-by-15-inch rectangle. Transfer pastry to prepared sheet. Spread filling in a 3-inch strip down the center of the pastry. Drop jam on top of filling; gently spread to evenly cover. Fold pastry edges in on either side, overlapping by at least 1 inch in the center. Pick up ends of the folded strip; bring them together to form into an oval. Pinch the edges to seal. Flip the oval so the seam side is down; press down on the pastry to slightly flatten. Bake 22 minutes, until light-golden brown. Transfer to a wire rack to cool.

For icing:

1. In a bowl, whisk powdered sugar, vanilla and enough milk to reach drizzling consistency. Drizzle over cooled pastry.

Double Swiss Omelet

An omelet makes a fine meal, regardless of the hour of day. If chard isn't available, substitute spinach (the cooking time will be shorter).

Serves 2

- 2 tablespoons olive oil, divided
- 1 small shallot, minced
- 1 small bunch Swiss chard, trimmed and inner ribs removed
- ¼ cup water
- 1 clove garlic, minced
- ½ cup Swiss cheese, shredded
- 5 large eggs
- Salt and black pepper

TIP: Wait to add the chard mixture until just before folding the omelet. Adding it earlier will make the omelet watery.

1. Warm 1 tablespoon oil in a 9-inch nonstick skillet over medium-low heat. Add shallots; cook 1 minute, until softened, stirring. Add chard and ¼ cup water; let the mixture sit in the pan 2 minutes to wilt down. Cook 8 minutes, until tender, stirring occasionally. Add garlic; cook 30 seconds, stirring. Transfer mixture to a medium bowl. Stir in cheese.
2. In a medium bowl, beat eggs, salt and pepper. Wipe out skillet with a paper towel; add remaining 1 tablespoon oil and set over medium-high heat. Once the pan is hot, add eggs. Let the pan sit for 5 seconds, until the omelet edges begin to set. Using a spatula, draw the lightly cooked egg to the center of the pan. Tilt the pan to the side so the uncooked egg runs to the bare spot at the edge of the pan. Repeat this process all around the edge of the pan until the omelet is just set but still moist in the center.
3. Gently drop the chard filling evenly over half the omelet. Cook 30 seconds to melt the cheese. Run the spatula quickly along the side of the omelet to loosen the edges. Jerk the pan sharply away from you a few times; the omelet should slide up the far side of the pan. Tilt the pan, resting the bottom of the pan on a serving plate. Slide the omelet onto the plate, using the spatula to fold over the omelet.

Creamiest Broccoli and Cheddar Scramble

Easy, cheesy and quick enough to make on a busy weekday. Make it once and you won't need a recipe the next time.

- 1 stalk broccoli, stalk and florets thinly sliced (about 2 cups)
- ½ cup water
- 8 large eggs
- ⅓ cup half-and-half
- 1 scallion, thinly sliced
- Salt and black pepper
- 2 tablespoons unsalted butter
- 2 ounces cream cheese, cubed and at room temperature
- 1 cup cheddar cheese, shredded or cubed

TIP: Make sure the broccoli florets are thinly sliced so they cook through in the short cooking time.

1. Stir-fry broccoli in a large nonstick skillet over medium-high heat for 1 minute. Add ½ cup water; cover pan and cook 2 minutes, until broccoli is crisp-tender. Drain off any water.
2. Meanwhile, in a large bowl, whisk eggs, half-and-half, scallions, salt and pepper. Add broccoli. Place skillet back over medium heat; add butter until melted. Pour in egg mixture and scramble to desired doneness. Remove from heat; stir in cream cheese and cheddar until melted and blended.

Breakfast Burritos for Two

Serve these hearty, flavorful burritos for any meal—
breakfast, brunch, lunch or dinner.

Serves 2

- 2 tablespoons olive oil, divided
- 1 small onion, diced
- 1 cup canned black beans, drained
- ½ teaspoon ground cumin
- Salt and black pepper
- 6 large eggs
- 1 cup Mexican blend cheese, shredded
- 2 burrito-sized flour tortillas, warmed

Garnishes

- Sour cream
- Prepared salsa
- Tomato, chopped
- Avocado, diced
- Fresh cilantro, chopped

TIP: Warming the tortillas makes them easier to fill and roll.

1. Warm 1 tablespoon of the oil in a large nonstick skillet over medium heat. Add onions; cook 4 minutes, until softened, stirring. Add beans, cumin, salt and pepper; cook 1 minute, until warmed through; transfer to a bowl. Wipe out pan with a paper towel.
2. Warm the remaining tablespoon oil in the same skillet over medium heat. In a large bowl, whisk eggs, salt and pepper. Add eggs to the hot pan; let sit 3 seconds, then scramble to desired doneness. Stir in cheese and remove from heat.
3. Lay tortillas on countertop. Spoon half the eggs in the center of each tortilla. Top with black-bean mixture, then toppings as desired. Roll up.

Heirloom Tomato and Goat Cheese Quiche

Heirloom tomatoes taste fantastic when they're ripe, but they aren't always available. Beefsteak or hothouse tomatoes make a fine substitute.

Serves 4

Crust

- 1¼ cups all-purpose flour
- 2 tablespoons cornstarch
- Pinch of salt
- 6 tablespoons unsalted butter, diced
- 1 large egg

Filling

- 2 large eggs
- ⅔ cup whole milk
- Salt and black pepper
- 4 ounces goat cheese, thinly sliced
- 2 medium ripe tomatoes, thinly sliced

TIP: This recipe works in a tart pan or a pie tin. The pie tin won't be as full as the tart pan.

For crust:

1. Preheat oven to 375°F. In a food processor, pulse flour, cornstarch and salt until combined. Add butter; pulse until dough resembles coarse meal. Add egg; pulse just until dough comes together. Dump dough onto a lightly floured surface. Form dough into a ball; roll the dough out to a 12-inch circle. Place the dough in a 9-inch fluted tart pan (or pie tin); press to fit bottom and up sides of pan. Refrigerate for 30 minutes.

For filling:

1. Remove crust from the refrigerator. In a large glass measuring cup, whisk eggs, milk, salt and pepper. Arrange slices of goat cheese in the crust; top with tomato slices, arranged in a circle. Pour egg filling into crust, filling to the top. Bake 45 minutes, until filling is puffed up and golden.

Spinach and Gruyère Strata

This rich and cheesy make-ahead casserole is perfect for cool-weather entertaining.

Serves 8

- 2 tablespoons unsalted butter, plus additional for greasing pan
- 1 medium onion, chopped
- ½ pound cremini or button mushrooms, sliced
- Salt and black pepper
- 8 cups cubed (¾ inch) challah or brioche bread
- 2 cups (about 6 ounces) Gruyère or Jarlsberg cheese, shredded
- 1 cup Parmesan cheese, grated
- 1 package (10 ounces) frozen spinach, thawed and drained of excess liquid
- 2½ cups whole milk
- 9 large eggs
- ½ teaspoon dry mustard powder

TIP: Don't worry about making the layers perfect—everything bakes together into one pan of creamy deliciousness.

1. Butter a 9-by-13-inch glass baking pan. Melt butter in a large cast-iron or heavy skillet over medium heat. Add onions and mushrooms; season with salt and pepper. Cook 8 minutes, until mushrooms release their liquid, stirring often.
2. Spread about one-third of the bread cubes in the prepared baking pan. Top with half of each cheese, half of the mushroom mixture and half of the spinach leaves. Top with one-third of the bread and the remaining mushrooms, spinach and cheese. Top everything with the remaining one-third of the bread.
3. In a large bowl, whisk milk, eggs, mustard powder, salt and pepper until blended. Pour evenly over casserole. Cover with plastic wrap and chill strata for at least 8 or up to 24 hours.
4. Remove strata from the refrigerator at least 30 minutes before baking. Preheat oven to 350°F. Bake, uncovered, 40 to 45 minutes, until golden and cooked through. Let stand 10 minutes before serving.

Denise's Bacon & Egg Breakfast Casserole

This hearty casserole will warm the hearts and bellies of the whole family. Use boiling potatoes, like Yukon Gold, for recipes like this one, where you want the potato to retain its shape when cooked.

- 2 strips bacon
- 3 medium Yukon Gold or white potatoes, cut into ½-inch dice (about 3 cups)
- 1 medium onion, diced
- 1 red pepper, diced
- Salt and black pepper
- 8 large eggs
- 1 cup whole milk
- 2 cups cheddar cheese, shredded

MAKE-AHEAD TIP: You can prepare the recipe just to the point of baking, cover and refrigerate for up to 24 hours. Let stand for 30 minutes at room temperature before baking.

1. Preheat oven to 350°F. Lightly oil a 9-by-13-inch baking pan.
2. Cook bacon in a large heavy skillet over medium-low heat until crisp. Drain on a paper towel–lined plate; crumble. Add potatoes, onions and red peppers to drippings in the pan; season with salt and pepper and cook 12 minutes, until golden and softened, stirring often. (Potatoes will not be completely cooked.)
3. In a large bowl, whisk eggs, milk, salt and pepper until thoroughly blended. Stir in cheese, crumbled bacon and potato mixture from the skillet. Pour mixture into prepared baking pan. Bake 40 minutes, or until the eggs are firm and the top is golden.

Autumn Corn Johnnycakes

These savory cakes make a special breakfast treat with maple syrup, or a change-of-pace dinner served with sausage links.

Makes about 14

- 2 large eggs
- 4 large ears corn
- ½ cup Monterey Jack cheese, shredded
- ½ cup whole milk
- 2 tablespoons fresh chives, chopped
- 3 tablespoons unsalted butter, melted and divided
- 1 cup all-purpose flour
- 1 teaspoon baking soda
- ¾ teaspoon salt

Garnishes

- Butter
- Maple syrup

TIP: If your corn is super-fresh, it will release its sweet juices when grated—adding extra flavor to the cakes.

1. Preheat oven to 200°F. Place a baking sheet in the oven to warm. In a large bowl, whisk eggs until blended. Using a box grater set inside the same bowl, grate the corn kernels into the bowl with the eggs. Fold in cheese, milk, chives and 2 tablespoons of the melted butter until combined. Fold in flour, baking soda and salt until blended.
2. Heat remaining tablespoon of melted butter in a large nonstick skillet over medium heat. Working in batches, drop batter in ¼ cupfuls into the hot pan. Cook for 5 minutes, flipping once, until lightly browned on both sides. Transfer cakes to the warmed sheet in the oven. Repeat with the remaining batter. Serve with butter and syrup.

Sweet Potato Hash with Italian Sausage

This hash is endlessly adaptable. Use any cheese you like. Omit the sausage or eggs if you don't want them. Anyway you make it—you'll love it.

- 2 large sweet potatoes (about 2 pounds), peeled and cut into small dice
- 2 tablespoons olive oil
- 2 tablespoons unsalted butter
- 1 medium onion, thinly sliced
- 3 cloves garlic, minced
- 2 tablespoons fresh rosemary, chopped
- ½ teaspoon paprika
- Salt and black pepper
- 8 ounces sweet Italian sausage, removed from casing and crumbled
- 4 large eggs
- 1 cup cheddar cheese, shredded

TIP: You can substitute dried rosemary for fresh, just use half as much.

1. Place diced sweet potatoes in a shallow, microwave-safe bowl with just enough water to barely cover. Cover bowl and microwave 4 minutes, until tender. Drain.
2. Preheat oven to 400°F. Warm oil and butter in a large cast-iron or heavy skillet over medium heat. Add onions, garlic, rosemary, paprika and drained potatoes. Season with salt and pepper and cook 10 minutes, until tender, stirring. Increase heat to medium-high; cook 5 more minutes, until crisp and cooked through, stirring often.
3. Meanwhile, in a medium skillet over medium-high heat, cook the sausage 10 minutes, until browned and starting to crisp. Drain any excess fat.
4. Mound sausage in the center of the hash in the cast-iron skillet. Make four wells in the hash and crack an egg into each well. Sprinkle with salt and pepper. Transfer to oven; bake 10 minutes, until potatoes are hot and eggs are baked through. Sprinkle with cheese.

Cast-Iron Skillet Buttermilk Cornbread

It's so easy to bake and serve this homey cornbread in a rustic cast-iron skillet. If you don't own one, use a 9-inch cake pan.

- 1 cup all-purpose flour
- ¾ cup cornmeal
- 1 tablespoon baking powder
- 2 teaspoons salt
- 1 cup buttermilk
- 4 tablespoons unsalted butter, melted, plus 1 tablespoon for pan
- ¼ cup pure maple syrup or honey
- 1 large egg
- 1½ cups corn kernels
- ¾ cup cheddar cheese, grated, plus extra for topping
- 2 tablespoons fresh chives, chopped

TIP: Serve cornbread warm or at room temperature.

1. Preheat oven to 350°F. Place a 9-inch cast-iron skillet in the oven to warm.
2. In a medium bowl, combine flour, cornmeal, baking powder and salt. In another bowl, whisk buttermilk, 4 tablespoons melted butter, maple syrup and egg until frothy and blended. Fold in dry ingredients, then corn, cheese and chives.
3. Remove pan from the oven; add the remaining tablespoon of butter and swirl it around to melt. Scrape batter into the hot pan; smooth the top. Sprinkle with additional cheese. Bake 25 to 30 minutes, until just firm to the touch and browned on the edges.

Carrot Cake Muffins

Perfect for brunch or bake sales,
this big-batch nutty muffin will please the whole crowd.

Makes 16

- 2½ cups all-purpose flour
- 1 teaspoon baking powder
- 1 teaspoon baking soda
- 1 teaspoon ground cinnamon
- ½ teaspoon ground ginger
- ½ teaspoon salt
- ¾ cup vegetable oil
- 4 tablespoons (½ stick) unsalted butter, at room temperature
- 1 cup granulated sugar
- 3 large eggs
- 2 teaspoons pure vanilla extract
- 1 ripe banana, mashed
- 1 cup carrots, grated (about 2 carrots)
- 1 tart apple, unpeeled and shredded
- ½ cup pecans or walnuts, chopped
- ½ cup sweetened coconut, shredded
- ½ cup dried cranberries

TIP: Transform these muffins into cupcakes by topping them with cream-cheese icing.

1. Preheat oven to 375°F. Line 16 muffin cups with paper liners. In a large bowl, whisk flour, baking powder, baking soda, cinnamon, ginger and salt.
2. In a large bowl with an electric mixer on high speed, cream oil, butter and sugar until combined. Beat in the eggs, one at a time, until blended. Beat in vanilla, banana, carrots and apple. Remove from mixer; fold in dry ingredients just until blended. Fold in nuts, coconut and cranberries.
3. Divide batter evenly among muffin cups. Bake 22 minutes, until golden but still just slightly undercooked in the center. Transfer to a wire rack to cool completely.

Elephant Ear Pull-Apart Bread

Dough

- 4 tablespoons (½ stick) unsalted butter, plus additional for buttering bowl and greasing pan
- ⅓ cup whole milk
- ¼ cup water
- 1 teaspoon vanilla extract
- 2¾ cups all-purpose flour, divided, plus additional for pan and rolling out
- ¼ cup granulated sugar
- 1 envelope (2¼ teaspoons) active dry yeast
- ½ teaspoon salt
- 2 large eggs, at room temperature

Filling

- 1 cup light-brown sugar
- 1 tablespoon ground cinnamon
- 4 tablespoons (½ stick) unsalted butter, melted

TIP: Bread tastes best the day it's made, but you can complete the recipe through step 5, then refrigerate the dough overnight. Let the dough sit at room temperature at least 30 minutes before baking.

Finger food! Serve this fun sweet bread at a party and let your guests peel off their pieces.

Makes 1 loaf

---

1. In a small saucepan, warm butter and milk until butter melts. Stir in ¼ cup water and vanilla. Let sit for 5 minutes, until just warm.
2. In a large bowl with an electric mixer on high speed, mix 2 cups of the flour, sugar, yeast and salt. With mixer speed on low, beat in warm butter mixture and eggs until combined. Dough will be sticky. Add remaining ¾ cup flour and beat until a wet dough forms. Scoop dough into a buttered bowl. Flip dough to coat; cover tightly with plastic and a dishcloth. Let rise in a warm place for at least 1 hour, until doubled in size.
3. Butter and lightly flour a 9-by-5-inch baking pan. Lightly press on risen dough to deflate; scrape onto a well-floured surface. Roughly knead a few times, then roll out into a 12-by-20-inch rectangle. Let dough sit 5 minutes.
4. Meanwhile, in a small bowl, mix brown sugar and cinnamon. Using a pastry brush, brush the entire surface of the dough with melted butter. Sprinkle with the sugar-cinnamon mixture. Using a sharp knife, slice the dough vertically into 6 equal strips. Stack strips on top of each other. Cut this stack into six equal squares. You will have 6 stacks of 6 squares.
5. Pick up each square stack and place it on its side in the prepared pan, like arranging books on a shelf. You may need to push the dough back in order to fit in all the stacks. Cover the pan with a dish towel and let it rise for 30 minutes.
6. Meanwhile, preheat oven to 350°F. Uncover the pan; bake 35 minutes, until golden brown and baked through. Let the bread cool in pan for 10 minutes. Run a metal spatula around the edges of the bread to release it from the pan. Invert the bread onto a wire rack.

Pumpkin Spice Latte Muffins

Celebrate the flavors of fall (and a popular coffee shop order!) with these spicy muffins.

Makes 9

Muffins

- 1 cup all-purpose flour
- 1 teaspoon baking powder
- ½ teaspoon baking soda
- 2 teaspoons pumpkin-pie spice
- 1 teaspoon ground cinnamon
- ½ teaspoon salt
- 2 large eggs
- ½ cup vegetable oil
- ½ cup light-brown sugar
- ½ cup granulated sugar
- 1 cup solid-pack pumpkin (not pumpkin-pie mix)

Glaze

- 2 teaspoons instant espresso powder
- 1½ tablespoons hot coffee
- ½ cup powdered sugar

TIP: Any unflavored vegetable oil will work in the recipe.

For muffins:

1. Preheat oven to 350°F. Line 9 muffin cups with paper liners. In a large bowl, whisk flour, baking powder, baking soda, pumpkin-pie spice, cinnamon and salt. In another large bowl, whisk eggs, oil, both sugars and pumpkin until blended. Fold in dry ingredients just until blended. Do not overmix.
2. Divide batter evenly among muffin cups. Bake 20 minutes, until firm on top but still just slightly soft in the center. Transfer to wire rack to cool completely.

For glaze:

1. In a small bowl, whisk espresso powder and hot coffee until powder is dissolved. Whisk in powdered sugar, a little at a time, to drizzling consistency. Drizzle in a zigzag pattern over cooled muffins.

Blueberry Muffin Coffee Cake

This gorgeous cake will make an impressive centerpiece at your next brunch.

Serves 12

Cake

- 2½ cups all-purpose flour, plus additional for coating blueberries
- 2 teaspoons baking powder
- 1 teaspoon salt
- 1 cup (2 sticks) unsalted butter, at room temperature, plus additional for greasing pan
- 2 cups granulated sugar
- Zest of 1 lemon, chopped
- 3 large eggs, at room temperature
- 2 teaspoons pure vanilla extract
- ¾ cup buttermilk or plain yogurt
- 3 cups blueberries

Topping

- ¼ cup granulated sugar
- 1 teaspoon ground cinnamon

TIP: Tossing the blueberries with flour ensures that they don't sink to the bottom of the cake during baking.

1. Preheat oven to 350°F. Grease and flour a 10-cup tube pan, preferably one with a removable bottom. In a medium bowl, whisk flour, baking powder and salt until blended.
2. In a large bowl with an electric mixer on high speed, cream butter, sugar and lemon zest for about 5 minutes, until light and fluffy. Add eggs, one at a time, beating well after each addition. Beat in vanilla. Reduce speed to low, then alternately add dry ingredients and buttermilk, beginning and ending with the flour mixture. Stop and scrape the sides of the bowl. Beat another few seconds until combined. Do not overmix.
3. In a medium bowl (you can use the same one the dry ingredients were mixed in), combine blueberries with a fistful of flour; toss to coat. Remove batter from the mixer; fold in blueberries until just blended. Scoop batter into prepared pan.
4. In a small bowl, whisk sugar and cinnamon; sprinkle over the batter. Bake 55 to 60 minutes, until a toothpick inserted in the center comes out clean. Transfer to a wire rack to cool. Run a metal spatula around the edges of the cake to loosen from the pan. Carefully remove the pan sides. Let the cake cool completely before releasing the cake from the pan.

Jo's Bar Applesauce-Stuffed French Toast

This clever baked French toast recipe means you don't have to stand at the stove cooking toast to order. We cheated a bit—the applesauce isn't exactly stuffed into the bread; rather, it's nestled between the baking slices.

- 7 thick slices raisin or white sandwich bread
- 3 tablespoons unsalted butter, at room temperature
- ¼ cup granulated sugar mixed with 1 tablespoon ground cinnamon
- ½ cup applesauce
- 1½ cups whole milk
- 3 large eggs
- 1 teaspoon pure vanilla extract
- Pinch of salt

Garnishes

- Whipped cream
- Maple syrup
- Powdered sugar

TIP: Use whatever bread your family likes, but make sure it's not a thin-sliced variety.

1. Preheat oven to 400°F. Butter an 8-by-8-inch baking pan.
2. Spread one side of each bread slice with butter; sprinkle with cinnamon-sugar mixture. Place bread on the baking sheet and bake 6 minutes, until toasted, flipping once. Reduce oven temperature to 350°F. Cut 3 slices in half. Lay the remaining 4 slices down the length of the pan, arranging them in an overlapping column. Fit half the slices around the edges of the pan to even out the height of the slices. Use a tablespoon to spoon the applesauce in between the slices, so that applesauce is completely covered by the toast.
3. In a medium bowl, whisk milk, eggs, vanilla and salt. Pour evenly over the toast slices. Let the toast sit for at least 15 minutes (or cover and refrigerate overnight). Bake 25 minutes, or until filling is just set. Serve hot, with garnishes as desired.

Caramel Apple Scones

Two classic fall flavors combine in this buttery breakfast treat.

Makes 4

Scones

- 1 tablespoon unsalted butter
- 2 baking apples (about ⅔ pound), peeled and cut into ¾-inch chunks
- Cinnamon sugar, as needed
- 1½ cups all-purpose flour
- ⅓ cup granulated sugar, plus additional for sprinkling
- 1½ teaspoons baking powder
- ¼ teaspoon salt
- 6 tablespoons cold unsalted butter, diced
- ¼ cup heavy cream
- 1 large egg

Glaze

- 2 tablespoons unsalted butter
- ¼ cup light-brown sugar
- 1 tablespoon whole milk
- ¼ cup powdered sugar

TIP: Mix the batter only until combined—overmixing makes for heavy scones.

For scones:

1. Preheat oven to 375°F. Line a baking sheet with parchment paper or a nonstick cooking pad. Melt butter in a medium skillet over medium heat. Add apple chunks and a palmful of cinnamon sugar; cook 3 minutes, until lightly browned and softened, stirring often.
2. In the bowl of an electric mixer on low speed, mix flour, sugar, baking powder and salt. Add diced butter, cream and egg. Mix on low speed just until batter comes together. Do not overmix. Remove from mixer; gently fold in apple chunks.
3. Scrape batter onto a lightly floured countertop. Form dough into a 6-inch round. Cut into 4 large wedges and transfer to prepared baking sheet at least 2 inches apart. Sprinkle wedges with additional sugar. Bake 27 to 30 minutes, until golden and just firm. Transfer to a wire rack to cool.

For glaze:

1. Melt butter in a small saucepan over medium-low heat. Stir in brown sugar. Bring to a simmer; simmer 2 minutes, until deep brown but not scorched, swirling mixture in pan as it cooks. Stir in milk (mixture will boil vigorously). Remove from heat; let cool at least 20 minutes. Whisk in powdered sugar until glaze forms. Drizzle over cooled scones.

CHAPTER 8

Greg grabbed Ana Raquel by the hand and led her out of the trailer. They both turned and saw that a large SUV had backed into the front corner of the trailer. The outside was ripped and cracked, but more upsetting was the big buckle in the frame.

Ana Raquel pulled free of his hold and moved toward the damage. A man in his thirties jumped out of the SUV and hurried over.

"I'm sorry," he said, his voice thick with anguish. "I have allergies. I sneezed and my foot slipped and I hit the gas instead of the brake. Are you okay?" He barely stopped speaking for Ana Raquel's nod. "I have insurance. I'm going to call my agent right now."

He pulled out a card from his wallet and started to dial on his cell.

The rational side of her brain knew that the trailer could be fixed. That while the frame damage meant more time in the shop, nothing was irreparable. But her heart whimpered about another truth. That by the time the repairs were done, the street food season would be over. Instead of ending things with a fun weeklong party of different dishes, as she'd planned, she would be forced to simply call it a season.

A crowd began to gather. This was Fool's Gold and everyone's business was fair game. There was also plenty of concern as people she knew hurried forward to make sure she was okay.

"We weren't hurt," Greg said, moving close and lightly putting his hand on her shoulder. "We were in the trailer when it happened. It rocked some, but we're fine."

Ana Raquel nodded because she was afraid that if she started to speak, she would begin to cry. She told herself that one great summer was enough. That she would have the trailer back for next year.

Greg shifted his hand so he had his arm around her. When the tourist who had backed into her started giving her his insurance info, Greg was the one who wrote it down. When the tow truck showed up, he helped her make sure all the propane lines were turned off and together they packed up the perishables. Less than an hour later, Ana Raquel watched as her dream was towed away.

Her little red truck, the one she used to pull her trailer, looked naked there on the street. There was a flyer for her business on a nearby pole. As she watched, a gust of wind caught it and tugged the paper free of its anchor. The sheet disappeared up into the sky.

"What on earth happened?"

"Are you okay?"

The familiar voices had her turning. Her two sisters, Dellina and Fayrene, hurried up to her. They reached for her and hugged her close.

"Are you hurt?" Dellina asked.

"Tourists are idiots," Fayrene muttered.

She let their care and concern wash over her. Tomorrow she would be rational about what had happened. Today she was going to wallow.

She sniffed, then stepped back. "How did you know what happened?"

"Greg called me," Dellina said. "I called Fayrene."

Greg had taken charge, but in a good way, she thought. She turned to thank him, but he'd disappeared into the crowd, leaving her in the capable arms of her family.

Chapter 9 begins on page 178

fall

Casseroles and Soups

Roasted Tomato Soup with Cheddar Crostini

Sure, you could open a can of tomato soup, but every now and then it's a treat to make your own. Cheesy crostini add a nice crunch.

Serves 6

Soup

- 3 pounds plum tomatoes, cut into large chunks
- 2 large cloves garlic, peeled and smashed
- 1 tablespoon olive oil
- 1 large shallot, minced (about ¼ cup)
- ½ teaspoon dried thyme or oregano
- 1 can (14¾ ounces) reduced-sodium chicken broth
- ¼ cup whole milk
- 2 tablespoons dry sherry
- Salt and black pepper

Crostini

- 3 tablespoons unsalted butter, at room temperature
- ½ skinny baguette, thinly sliced on the diagonal to make 12 crostini
- 12 thin slices sharp cheddar cheese

TIP: Roasting time will depend on the size of your tomatoes.

For soup:

1. Preheat oven to 350°F. Line 2 rimmed baking sheets with foil. Place tomatoes, cut-side down, on prepared sheets. Add smashed garlic cloves to one pan. Roast 45 minutes, until tomatoes are very soft. Remove and let cool on a wire rack.
2. Meanwhile, warm oil in a Dutch oven or a large saucepan over medium-low heat. Add shallots; cook 4 minutes, until softened, stirring. Add roasted tomatoes, roasted garlic, thyme and broth; bring to a simmer and cook for 15 minutes, smashing tomatoes against the sides of the pot. Working in batches, transfer soup to a blender or food processor and purée until smooth. Return soup to pot; add milk and sherry and cook to warm through. Season to taste with salt and pepper.

For crostini:

1. Preheat oven to 350°F. Spread butter on both sides of bread slices; arrange on a baking sheet. Bake 5 minutes, until lightly golden. Remove from oven; cover each toast with a cheese slice. Bake until cheese melts.

Chilly Day White Bean, Kale and Sausage Soup

This is one of those set-it-and-forget-it recipes. Just throw the beans, herbs, garlic and broth in a pot and go about your business. In a few hours and a whirl of the blender, you've got a creamy bowl of heaven.

- 1 pound dried cannellini or Great Northern beans
- 5 cloves garlic, unpeeled
- 1 branch fresh rosemary
- 4 cups (1 quart) reduced-sodium chicken broth
- Salt and black pepper
- 2 cups coarsely chopped kale or Swiss chard
- 1 pound (4 large links) garlic and herb sausage, thickly sliced on the diagonal

TIP: Be sure to trim the woody stems from the leafy green you use. Or substitute baby spinach, which will wilt in even less time.

1. Place beans in a large bowl; cover with water and refrigerate overnight.
2. In a Dutch oven or a large saucepan, combine drained beans, garlic, rosemary and broth to cover by at least 4 inches. Bring to a boil over high heat. Reduce heat, cover and simmer 3 hours, until beans are tender, stirring occasionally. Add water, if needed, during cooking time. Remove garlic and rosemary. Season with salt and pepper to taste.
3. Working in batches, purée soup to desired consistency. Return to the pot over medium heat. Add kale and sausage; cook 10 minutes, until kale wilts and sausage is warmed through.

Baked Potato Leek Soup

All the wonderful flavors of a baked potato in a soup!

Soup

- 4 strips bacon
- 2 tablespoons unsalted butter
- 2 pounds Yukon Gold or boiling potatoes, cut into ¾-inch chunks
- 4 leeks, white and light green parts, cleaned then thinly sliced
- Salt and black pepper
- 2 cans (14¾-ounce size) reduced-sodium chicken broth (or about 4 cups)
- ½ cup half-and-half or whole milk
- ½ cup shredded Monterey Jack or white cheddar cheese

Garnishes

- Sliced scallions
- Sour cream
- Cheese, shredded

TIP: Purée the soup as smooth or as chunky as you like.

1. Preheat oven to 400°F. In a large Dutch oven, cook bacon until crisp. Drain on a paper towel–lined plate; coarsely chop.
2. Melt butter in drippings in the same pot over medium heat. Stir in potatoes and leeks. Season with salt and pepper. Place in the oven and roast 45 minutes, until tender, turning with a spatula occasionally.
3. Remove pot from the oven; place over medium-low heat. Stir in 1 can (about 2 cups) broth. Using an immersion blender, blend soup to desired chunkiness. (Alternatively, add soup to a food processor and purée in batches.) Stir in the remaining can (about 2 cups) broth and blend as above. Stir in half-and-half and cheese and cook to warm through and incorporate, stirring often. Season to taste with salt and pepper. Serve with garnishes.

Coconut Acorn Squash Bisque

Coconut oil imparts a nice sweetness to this creamy, good-for-you soup.

Serves 6

- 2 acorn squashes, halved
- 3 tablespoons olive or coconut oil, divided
- 2 carrots, thinly sliced
- 1 onion, diced
- 2 cloves garlic, minced
- ¼ teaspoon ground cumin
- Pinch of ground coriander
- ½ cup white wine
- 3 cups reduced-sodium chicken broth
- 1 can (14 ounces) coconut milk
- Salt and black pepper

Garnishes

- Sour cream or yogurt
- Fresh cilantro, chopped

TIP: This is a great squash roasting method to commit to memory for an anytime side dish.

1. Preheat oven to 400°F. Rub cut sides of squash with 1 tablespoon of the oil. Place squash, cut-side down, on a baking sheet. Roast 45 minutes, until soft. Remove from oven; let cool slightly.
2. Warm the remaining 2 tablespoons oil in a Dutch oven or a large saucepan over medium heat. Add carrots and onions; cook 8 minutes, stirring. Add garlic, cumin and coriander; cook 30 seconds, stirring. Stir in wine; cook 2 minutes until alcohol cooks off. Spoon squash purée out of the skin and add to the pot, smashing squash against the sides of the pot. Stir in broth until blended. Cook 15 minutes, stirring occasionally. Working in batches, transfer soup to a blender and purée until smooth. (Alternatively, purée soup in the pot using an immersion blender.) Return soup to the pot. Stir in coconut milk; cook 5 minutes, until blended and warmed through. Season to taste with salt and pepper. Garnish with sour cream and cilantro.

Black Bean Soup with Lime Cream

Chipotle chilies add a smoky heat to this satisfying soup. You'll find them in the Mexican food aisle, packaged in adobo sauce. Make sure to seed the peppers before chopping and adding to the soup.

Soup

- 1 tablespoon olive oil
- 1 large red onion, chopped
- 1 red bell pepper, chopped
- 4 cloves garlic, minced
- 1–2 teaspoons canned chipotle chilies, seeded and chopped
- 1½ tablespoons ground cumin
- 1 bag (16 ounces) dried black beans
- 3 cans (14¾-ounce size) reduced-sodium chicken broth
- 2 tablespoons fresh lime juice
- Salt and black pepper

Lime cream garnish and chips

- Sour cream
- Lime juice and lime zest
- Lime-flavored tortilla chips

MAKE-AHEAD TIP: This soup tastes even better the next day. It will keep for several days in the fridge and freezes perfectly.

For soup:

1. Warm oil in a large skillet or Dutch oven over medium heat. Add onions and bell peppers; cook 6 minutes, until softened, stirring often. Stir in garlic, chipotles and cumin; cook 30 seconds, stirring. Pour mixture into 6-quart slow cooker. Stir in beans and broth. Cover and cook on high until beans are very tender, about 5 to 6 hours. (Alternatively, bring to a simmer in same pot and cook 2 ½ hours over medium-low heat, adding water if mixture seems too dry.)
2. Working in batches, transfer soup to a blender; purée until smooth. Return purée to cooker. Stir in lime juice, salt and pepper to taste.

For cream:

1. In a small bowl, whisk sour cream, lime juice and zest to taste. Garnish servings with cream. Serve with lime chips.

Homemade Chunky Vegetable Soup

The rind from a wedge of Parmesan cheese adds rich flavor to this soup. The next time you've grated all the cheese from a rind, secure it in a resealable plastic bag and freeze it for your next soup.

- 1 tablespoon olive oil
- 2 leeks, thinly sliced and washed
- 1 stalk celery, thinly sliced
- 1 small zucchini, diced
- 1 small yellow squash, diced
- 1 can (28 ounces) whole plum tomatoes, drained and chopped
- 1 can (14½ ounces) reduced-sodium chicken broth
- 1 rind Parmesan cheese, about 3 inches by 1 inch
- Salt and black pepper
- 4 cups water, plus more if needed
- 1 bunch or bag (5 ounces) spinach, chopped (about 4 packed cups)
- 6 tablespoons Parmesan cheese, grated, for garnish

MAKE-AHEAD TIP: This soup is a great make-ahead meal. Refrigerate in an airtight container for 3 days or freeze for 1 month.

1. Warm oil in a large Dutch oven or saucepan over medium heat. Add leeks and celery; cook 5 minutes, stirring. Add zucchini, squash, tomatoes, broth, cheese rind, salt and pepper. Add 4 cups water; bring to a boil. Reduce heat to medium-low; simmer 30 minutes. Stir in spinach; cook 10 minutes, until vegetables are tender, stirring occasionally and adding water if needed. Remove cheese rind. Garnish servings with grated cheese.

Day-After Turkey and Wild Rice Chowder

Make this satisfying soup with turkey after Thanksgiving or with chicken anytime. Don't have a carcass? Use legs, wings or other meaty bones.

Broth

- 1 tablespoon unsalted butter
- 1 onion, chopped
- 1 stalk celery, chopped
- 1 turkey or chicken carcass, cut into 4 pieces, or any large poultry bones
- 3 cups white wine
- 5 cups low-sodium chicken broth

Soup

- 1 tablespoon unsalted butter
- 1 cup wild rice
- 3 carrots, peeled and chopped
- ¼ teaspoon dried sage
- ¼ teaspoon baking soda
- ¾ cup half-and-half
- ¼ cup all-purpose flour
- 3 cups chopped cooked turkey
- 1½ cups frozen peas, thawed
- Salt and black pepper

TIP: Adding baking soda to the soup reduces the cooking time by about 15 minutes.

For the broth:

1. Melt butter in a large Dutch oven over medium-high heat. Cook onions, celery, and turkey carcass until lightly browned, about 5 minutes. Add wine and chicken broth and simmer over medium-low heat for 1 hour. Strain broth, discarding solids. You should have about 6 cups.

For the soup:

1. Melt butter in the same pot (no need to clean) over medium heat. Add rice; cook 5 minutes, until rice begins to pop. Stir in warm broth, carrots, sage and baking soda. Bring to a boil. Reduce heat to low and simmer, covered, until rice is tender, about 1 hour. Add water if needed during cooking time.
2. In a small bowl, whisk half-and-half and flour until blended. Stir cream mixture into soup. Add turkey and peas; simmer 10 minutes to combine flavors and warm through. Season with salt and pepper.

Denise's Many-Layered Tamale Pie

The cornbread topping rises magically to make a golden crown over this Mexican-flavored casserole.

Tamale pie

- 1 pound ground beef
- 1 small red onion, chopped
- ½ jalapeño pepper, seeded and minced
- 2 tablespoons taco seasoning
- ¾ cup frozen corn, thawed
- 1 cup tomatoes, diced, canned or fresh
- ½ cup black olives, diced
- ¾ cup sharp cheddar cheese, shredded

Cornbread topping

- ¾ cup cornmeal
- ½ cup all-purpose flour
- 2 tablespoons granulated sugar
- 2 teaspoons baking powder
- 1 teaspoon salt
- 1 large egg
- ½ cup whole milk
- 3 tablespoons butter, melted
- ¼ cup cheddar cheese, shredded
- Sour cream, for garnish

For tamale pie:

1. Preheat oven to 375°F. In a heavy skillet over medium-high heat, cook beef, onions and jalapeños for 6 minutes, until browned, stirring often. Stir in taco seasoning and corn; cook 30 seconds, stirring. Scrape mixture into a 2-quart casserole or a 9-inch baking pan. Top with tomatoes, olives and ¾ cup cheese.

For topping:

1. In a bowl, whisk cornmeal, flour, sugar, baking powder and salt. In another bowl, whisk egg, milk and butter until blended. Make a well in the dry ingredients; pour in diced wet ingredients and stir just until blended. Spoon batter on top of shredded cheese in diced casserole. Sprinkle with ¼ cup cheese. Bake 30 minutes, until cornbread is baked and lightly golden around the edges. Top individual servings with sour cream, as desired.

TIP: Seeding the jalapeño ensures that it doesn't add too much heat to the dish.

Rich Red-Wine Beef Stew

- 3 strips bacon, sliced
- 5 tablespoons olive oil, divided
- 1 pound cremini or button mushrooms, thinly sliced
- 2½ pounds beef chuck, trimmed and cut into 1-inch chunks
- ⅓ cup all-purpose flour
- Salt and black pepper
- 1 cup red wine, divided
- 3 large carrots, sliced
- 2 stalks celery, sliced
- 1 large onion, chopped
- 3 cloves garlic, minced
- 1 teaspoon dried thyme or 2 teaspoons fresh thyme leaves, chopped
- 1 can (14¾ ounces) beef broth
- 1 can (28 ounces) whole plum tomatoes with juices
- 8 ounces egg noodles
- Butter, for serving

TIP: You can often buy beef chuck already cut and labeled "Beef for Stew." Check to make sure these chunks are the correct size—you may have to cut them further.

There is nothing as satisfying on a cold night as a hearty beef stew.
This recipe makes a big batch—freeze half for another night.

1. In a Dutch oven or a large ovenproof saucepan, cook bacon until crisp, stirring. Transfer to a large, shallow bowl; crumble. Add 1 tablespoon of the oil to drippings in the pan over medium-low heat. Cook mushrooms 10 minutes, until softened, stirring often. Using a slotted spoon, remove mushrooms to a bowl, retaining fat in the pot. Add 1 tablespoon oil to pan; increase heat to medium-high.
2. In a large bowl, toss beef chunks with flour, salt and pepper until coated. Working in 3 batches, add beef to the hot pan, cooking 8 minutes until browned on all sides, but not cooked through. Transfer to the bowl with the bacon. Pour ⅓ cup of the wine into the pan; stirring to scrape up browned bits in the pan. Using pot holders, pick up the pan and add any deglazing juices to the bowl with the browned beef. Repeat the process 2 more times with 1 tablespoon oil and beef, deglazing the pan each time with another ⅓ cup wine.
3. Add remaining tablespoon oil to the pan over medium-low heat. Add carrots, celery and onions; cook 8 minutes, until softened, stirring often. Add garlic and thyme; cook 30 seconds, stirring. Return beef, bacon and juices on the plate to the pot, along with broth and tomatoes. Bring to a simmer; partially cover and cook 2½ to 3 hours, until beef is very tender, stirring occasionally and adding water to pot as needed. Stir mushrooms into pot in the last 5 minutes of cooking.
4. About 20 minutes before the stew is done, cook noodles according to package directions. Drain and toss with butter. Serve the stew over the noodles.

Dinner Party Scalloped Potatoes

This golden pan of melty potatoes and bubbling cheese is sure to be the star of your next party.

Serves 12

- Butter, for greasing pan
- 2 cups shredded Gruyère or Jarlsberg cheese
- 1 cup Parmesan cheese, grated
- 4 pounds Idaho or baking potatoes, peeled and very thinly sliced
- Salt, black pepper and ground nutmeg
- 1 large shallot, minced
- 3 tablespoons all-purpose flour
- 3 cups whole milk

TIP: The casserole can be prepared completely up to 2 hours ahead. Rewarm in a 300°F oven for about 20 minutes.

1. Preheat oven to 400°F. Butter a 9-by-13-inch glass or ceramic baking dish. In a small bowl, toss cheeses until combined.
2. Arrange half the potatoes in prepared pan. Sprinkle generously with salt and lightly with pepper and nutmeg. Sprinkle all the shallots and flour and half the cheese over top. Cover with remaining potatoes and additional salt and pepper.
3. In a medium saucepan, bring milk just to a simmer. Pour warm milk evenly over the potatoes. Cover pan with buttered foil; bake 40 minutes. Uncover pan; sprinkle with remaining cheese and bake 45 minutes until potatoes are cooked through and cheese is bubbling. Let sit 15 minutes before serving.

Italian Sausage and Pepper Casserole

A nice change from pasta and rice, golden rounds of polenta top this one-pot country-style dish.

Serves 6

- 3 tablespoons olive oil, plus more for pan
- 1 pound sweet Italian sausage (removed from casings)
- 1 yellow onion, chopped
- 1 red pepper, chopped
- 4 cloves garlic, minced
- 1 tablespoon fresh oregano, chopped
- ½ teaspoon fennel seeds
- Salt and black pepper
- 1 can (28-ounce) crushed tomatoes
- 1 pound prepared polenta, cut into ½-inch slices
- ½ pound fresh mozzarella, thinly sliced

TIP: It's worth it to invest in a good cast-iron or heavy, ovenproof skillet for meals, like this one, that go from stovetop to broiler to table.

1. Warm 1 tablespoon of the oil in a large cast-iron or heavy, ovenproof skillet over medium heat. Add sausage; cook until browned, stirring often. Remove to a plate. Add remaining oil to drippings in the pan, still over medium heat. Cook onions and peppers 10 minutes, stirring often. Stir in garlic, oregano, fennel, salt and pepper; cook 1 minute, stirring. Add tomatoes, cover pan, reduce heat to low and simmer 20 minutes.
2. Preheat broiler. Arrange polenta slices on a baking sheet; broil 8 minutes until golden.
3. Arrange cooked polenta over the sausage mixture; top with cheese slices. Transfer skillet to the oven; broil 2 minutes, or until cheese melts. Cool 5 minutes before serving.

One-Pot Chicken Pasta with Broccoli and Sun-Dried Tomato Sauce

Check out this clever pasta cooking technique—
this is a one-pot wonder.

- 1½ pounds chicken tenders, halved lengthwise, or boneless, skinless chicken breast halves, cut into strips
- Salt and black pepper
- 1 tablespoon olive oil
- 1 tablespoon unsalted butter
- 4 cloves garlic, minced
- ½ cup sun-dried tomatoes packed in oil, chopped
- 12 ounces medium shells or gemelli pasta
- 3 cups reduced-sodium chicken broth
- 2 cups water
- 1 large broccoli stalk, stalks thinly sliced and florets cut small (about 4 cups)
- ½ cup half-and-half
- 1 teaspoon cornstarch
- 1¼ cups Parmesan cheese, grated
- 1 tablespoon fresh lemon juice

TIP: Dinner for a crowd—this recipe will serve at least 8.

1. Season chicken with salt and pepper. Warm oil and butter in a Dutch oven or a large skillet with at least 2-inch sides over medium-high heat. Add chicken; cook 8 minutes, until golden and almost cooked through, stirring often. Stir in garlic and sun-dried tomatoes; cook for 30 seconds, stirring. Transfer to a bowl.
2. Place the same skillet (no need to wash) over high heat. Add pasta, broth and 2 cups water. Bring to a boil and cook 14 minutes, or until most of the liquid is absorbed and pasta is almost tender. Add broccoli; cover pan and reduce heat to medium. Cook 2 minutes, until broccoli is crisp-tender.
3. In a small bowl, whisk half-and-half and cornstarch. Stir mixture into the pot, along with the Parmesan. Add chicken mixture and any juices from the bowl. Simmer 2 minutes, until the sauce has thickened and warmed through. Remove from heat; stir in lemon juice.

Sweet Potato and Spinach Gratin

This is a great make-ahead recipe for holiday entertaining. The gratin can be made through step 3. At that point, cover the pan with plastic wrap and refrigerate. Let casserole sit at room temperature for 30 minutes before continuing with the recipe.

- 5 tablespoons unsalted butter, divided, plus extra for greasing the pan
- 1 small onion, chopped
- 1 pound frozen spinach, thawed and squeezed dry
- 4 tablespoons all-purpose flour
- 3 cups whole milk
- 2 teaspoons fresh thyme leaves, chopped
- Pinch of ground nutmeg
- Salt and black pepper
- 2 medium sweet potatoes (about 1½ pounds), peeled and cut into very thin slices
- 2 cups Jarlsberg or Swiss cheese, shredded, and divided

TIP: Be sure to squeeze as much of the liquid as possible from the spinach before adding it to the pot.

1. Warm 1 tablespoon of the butter in a medium saucepan over medium heat. Add onions, cook 4 minutes, until softened, stirring often. Add spinach; cook until any liquid evaporates. Using a slotted spoon, transfer cooked spinach and onions to a bowl. Drain off any liquid remaining in the pot.
2. Melt the remaining 4 tablespoons butter in the same pan over medium-low heat. Sprinkle in flour, stirring until a paste forms. Slowly add milk, a little at a time, until incorporated. Cook 6 minutes, until thickened and bubbly. Remove from heat; stir in thyme, nutmeg, salt and pepper.
3. Preheat oven to 375°F. Butter a 9-by-13-inch glass baking pan. Spread half of the sweet potato slices in the pan. Sprinkle with salt, pepper, ½ cup of the cheese and half of the spinach mixture. Drizzle half of the white sauce over these layers. Continue with the remaining sweet potatoes, more salt, pepper, ½ cup cheese and then the remaining spinach. Pour the remaining sauce over the gratin. Sprinkle with the remaining 1 cup cheese.
4. Bake for 55 minutes, until golden and bubbly, and the sweet potatoes have cooked through. Let stand 10 minutes before serving.

Baked Ziti with Butternut Squash and Ricotta

Where is it written that baked pasta dishes have to be loaded with tomato sauce and cheese? This one stars creamy ricotta and sweet squash.

Serves 6

Vegetable oil, to grease the pan

1 pound ziti, penne or small shells pasta

1 bag (16 ounces) frozen puréed butternut squash, thawed

1 container (15 ounces) ricotta cheese

2 large eggs

Salt and black pepper

¾ cup Parmesan, grated, and divided

½ cup prepared basil pesto

TIP: Whole-milk ricotta is best for cooking. Low-fat varieties don't stand up to high heat as well.

1. Preheat oven to 375°F. Lightly oil a 9-by-13-inch glass baking dish.
2. Cook pasta 2 minutes less than package directions. Drain. Meanwhile, place squash in a metal colander; set colander over boiling pasta to warm through.
3. In a large bowl, whisk ricotta, warm squash, eggs, salt and pepper. Fold in the cooked pasta until coated. Stir in ¼ cup of the Parmesan.
4. Spoon mixture evenly into the prepared baking dish; dot with pesto and sprinkle with the remaining ½ cup Parmesan. Bake, uncovered, for 30 minutes, until lightly golden and warmed through. Let stand for 5 minutes before serving.

Mushroom and Three-Cheese Lasagna

This dish takes traditional lasagna to new heights. You won't miss the meat.

Sauce

- 2 tablespoons olive oil
- 2 tablespoons unsalted butter
- 1 medium onion, chopped
- 1 pound cremini or button mushrooms, sliced
- 4 cloves garlic, minced
- ⅔ cup white wine

Pasta

- 9 lasagna noodles

Filling

- 2 large eggs
- 1 egg yolk
- 1 container (15 ounces) ricotta cheese
- ½ cup Parmesan cheese, grated
- ¼ cup prepared pesto sauce
- Salt and black pepper

Topping

- Oil, to grease the pan
- 1 pound shredded mozzarella cheese
- ½ cup Parmesan cheese, grated

For sauce:

1. Warm oil and butter in a large heavy skillet or Dutch oven over medium heat. Add onions; cook 5 minutes, until softened, stirring. Add mushrooms and garlic; cover pan for 2 minutes. Uncover pan; cook 8 minutes, stirring, until mushrooms soften and release their liquid. Add wine; increase heat to medium-high and simmer 5 minutes, until liquid has reduced. Reduce heat to low and cook 8 minutes, until sauce is thick, adding water if needed to reach a saucy consistency.

For pasta and filling:

1. Meanwhile, cook pasta 2 minutes less than package directions. Drain and rinse with cold water, using fingers to separate the noodles. In a large bowl, whisk eggs and yolk until blended. Fold in ricotta, ½ cup Parmesan and pesto until combined. Season to taste with salt and pepper.

For topping and assembling the dish:

1. Preheat oven to 350°F. Lightly oil a 9-by-13-inch baking pan. Lay 3 noodles in the prepared pan. Cover with half the mushroom sauce, then half the ricotta filling. Top with 3 more noodles, then the remaining half of mushroom sauce and half of filling. Top with the remaining 3 noodles, mozzarella and ½ cup Parmesan. Cover lasagna with foil and bake 35 minutes. Uncover and bake 25 minutes longer, until sauce bubbles and cheese melts. Let stand 10 minutes before serving.

Baked Wild Mushroom Risotto

This method of baking risotto means you don't have to stand and stir the rice.

- ½ ounce dried porcini mushrooms, chopped
- 2 cups boiling water
- 2 tablespoons unsalted butter
- 1 large onion, chopped
- 2 cloves garlic, minced
- 1 carton (10 ounces) button mushrooms, sliced
- 1 small Portobello mushroom, chopped
- 2 teaspoons chopped fresh thyme leaves
- Salt and black pepper
- 1¼ cups Arborio or California short-grain white rice
- ½ cup dry white wine
- 2 cups reduced-sodium chicken or vegetable broth
- Swiss or Parmesan cheese, shredded, for garnish

TIP: Don't skip the dried porcini step—it adds a depth of mushroom flavor.

1. Preheat oven to 325°F. Rinse the dried porcini mushrooms lightly, to remove grit. Place dried mushrooms in a bowl; cover with 2 cups boiling water. Set aside.
2. Melt butter in a medium-heavy ovenproof saucepan over medium heat. Add onions and garlic; cook 6 minutes, until softened, stirring occasionally. Add button and Portobello mushrooms, thyme, salt and pepper; cook 8 minutes, until liquid is released and mushrooms are golden, stirring occasionally.
3. Drain dried mushrooms, reserving the liquid. Add the mushrooms to the pot; cook 1 minute, stirring. Add rice and cook 3 minutes, stirring a few times, until mixture is thick and dry. Increase heat; add wine, broth and reserved mushroom steeping liquid. Using a wooden spoon, scrape the bottom of the pan to release any browned bits. Bring to a simmer. Cover pan with a tight-fitting lid; place in oven and bake for 35 to 40 minutes, until rice is cooked through and liquid mostly evaporated. Let stand for 5 minutes. Garnish servings with cheese.

Curried Lentil and Sweet Potato Stew

Serve this vibrant and nutritious stew over rice.

Serves 6

- 2 tablespoons olive oil (or 1 tablespoon olive oil and 1 tablespoon coconut oil)
- 1 medium onion, chopped
- 3 cloves garlic, minced
- ½ inch piece fresh gingerroot, peeled and minced
- 2 teaspoons curry powder
- 1 teaspoon garam masala
- ½ jalapeño pepper, seeded and minced
- 2 cans (14 ¾-ounce size) reduced-sodium chicken or vegetable broth
- 2 medium sweet potatoes (about 1½ pounds), peeled and cut into ½-inch cubes (about 4 cups)
- 1 cup dried lentils
- 1 bay leaf
- Salt and black pepper
- ⅓ cup fresh cilantro, chopped
- 2 tablespoons fresh lime juice

1. Warm oil in a medium saucepan over medium heat. Add onions; cook 5 minutes, until softened, stirring. Add garlic, ginger, curry, garam masala and jalapeño. Cook 1 minute, stirring often.
2. Stir in broth, sweet potatoes, lentils, bay leaf, salt and pepper. Liquid should just cover vegetables; if it doesn't, add water to cover. Increase heat to high and bring to a boil; reduce heat, partially cover and simmer 40 minutes, until lentils are tender and sweet potatoes are cooked through. (Add water if needed during cooking time.)
3. Remove stew from heat. Remove bay leaf; stir in cilantro and lime juice.

TIP: For the sweetest flavor and the most tender texture, use the orange-fleshed sweet potatoes (sometimes mistakenly labeled as yams) for this recipe. Drier, less sweet, white-fleshed sweet potatoes cook up crumbly.

Pumpkin Bread Pudding

Serve this sweet casserole for breakfast, tea or dessert. The caramel sauce sends it over the top!

Pudding

- 6 tablespoons (¾ stick) unsalted butter, chopped
- 6 cups day-old challah or crusty bread, cut into 1-inch cubes
- 1½ cups whole milk
- 1 cup canned solid-pack pumpkin
- ¾ cup granulated sugar
- 2 large eggs, plus 1 egg yolk
- ½ teaspoon salt
- 1 teaspoon pumpkin-pie spice
- ½ teaspoon ground cinnamon
- Pinch of ground cloves
- Powdered sugar, for sprinkling

Caramel sauce

- 1¼ cups dark brown sugar
- ½ cup (1 stick) unsalted butter
- ½ cup heavy cream

TIP: Make sure to use solid-pack pumpkin, not pumpkin-pie mix.

For pudding:

1. Preheat oven to 350°F. Put butter in a 2-quart casserole; place in oven to melt. Remove pan from oven; add bread cubes and toss until coated.
2. In a medium bowl, whisk milk, pumpkin, sugar, eggs, egg yolk, salt and all spices; evenly pour over bread cubes. Bake 25 minutes, until set.

For caramel sauce:

1. In a medium-heavy saucepan over medium heat, whisk brown sugar and butter until butter melts. Whisk in cream and stir until sugar dissolves and sauce is smooth, about 3 minutes.
2. Sift powdered sugar over bread pudding. Serve warm with caramel sauce.

Sunday Dinner Chicken Potpie

Rich puff pastry covers this homey, filling potpie.
If you can't find it in your local store, use a prepared pie crust.

Serves 6

- 3 bone-in, skin-on chicken breast halves (about 3 pounds)
- 3 sprigs fresh thyme plus 2 teaspoons thyme leaves, chopped
- 8 cups water
- 6 tablespoons unsalted butter, chopped
- 1 large onion, diced
- 2 carrots, cut into small dice
- 6 tablespoons all-purpose flour
- 1 package (10 ounces) frozen peas, thawed
- ½ cup fresh Italian parsley, chopped
- Salt and black pepper
- 1 sheet frozen puff pastry, thawed
- 1 egg beaten with 1 tablespoon water, for egg wash

MAKE-AHEAD TIP: Make chicken filling one day in advance.

1. Place chicken breasts and thyme sprigs in a Dutch oven or a large saucepan. Add 8 cups water. Bring to a boil over high heat. Reduce heat; simmer 15 to 20 minutes, until cooked through. Remove chicken and place on a cutting board. Reserve cooking broth in a measuring cup; you need 5 cups. (Set aside extra broth for another use.) Let chicken cool slightly. Remove and discard skin and bones. Shred meat.
2. Melt butter in the same pot over medium heat (no need to clean). Add onions and carrots; cook 8 minutes, stirring often. Sprinkle in flour; cook 2 minutes, stirring until a paste forms. Pour in reserved cooking broth, a little at a time, stirring to incorporate after each addition. Bring to a simmer; cook 8 minutes, until thickened, stirring often. Remove from heat; stir in shredded chicken, peas, parsley, chopped thyme, salt and pepper.
3. Preheat oven to 375°F. Spoon filling into a 9-inch cast-iron skillet or a heavy, ovenproof casserole dish. Unfold thawed pastry crust on a lightly floured counter. Roll out to a 10-inch circle. Place pastry on top of the skillet, pressing around the edges to form a seal. Cut a hole in the center of the pastry to allow steam to escape. Brush dough with egg wash. Bake 25 to 30 minutes, until pastry is puffed and golden and filling is hot.

CHAPTER

The next day Ana Raquel found herself back at her spot for lunch. She had regulars who might not have heard about the accident and she wanted to explain why she was shutting down so early. She'd barely been able to sleep that night and when she did manage to doze off, she was awakened by nightmares of the accident.

It wasn't the damage that bothered her as much as having things taken out of her control. She tried telling herself the good news: no one had been hurt and she was grateful for that. But still... what about her dream? Next year seemed so far away.

She rounded the corner and found that her usual place had already been taken by a large SUV. One that looked familiar. As she pulled up behind it, she saw that Greg had set up a table just off the sidewalk with a big hand-lettered sign. It showed a crayon version of her trailer with a big bandage on the back corner. The notice above invited her customers to write in their best wishes.

More amazing were the stacks of sandwiches and salads he was setting out on the table. She got out of her car and hurried over to him.

"What is all this?" she asked.

Greg smiled at her. "I didn't want your regulars going hungry," he told her. "I went into the restaurant early and threw a few things together."

She felt her mouth drop open. "You didn't have to."

"I know. I wanted to. You were pretty upset yesterday."

She nodded. "Too upset to think of doing this. What a great idea." Her season didn't have to end so abruptly, she thought happily. She could make food at home and bring it here. While the menu wouldn't be so extensive, she had already made her cookies and muffins the night before.

"Thank you," she said, impulsively hugging him. "You're being really good to me. I appreciate it."

His body was warm against hers, she thought, suddenly aware of pressing against him with only a few layers of clothing between them. She felt the heat of him and found herself wanting something more than just a hug. She wanted to hang on and never let go and, at the same time, she found herself needing to cry.

Adrenaline, she told herself as she stepped back. Emotional residue from the accident.

"I don't know how to repay you for all this." She motioned to the sandwiches and salads.

"Send them up to my place for dinner."

He was joking, but she was serious as she said she would. She would tell everyone to go there, she thought. And she would mention what a nice guy he was.

He walked toward his SUV. "We still need to get going on our cookbook planning," he called over his shoulder.

"Tomorrow at three," she promised. "Café kitchen."

"I look forward to it."

"Me, too," she whispered. Because she did. A lot.

Chapter 10 begins on page 181

CHAPTER 10

The next couple of months passed in a blur. Ana Raquel and Greg argued and negotiated their way through recipes, organization and bonus material. The town came through with recipe suggestions. Ana Raquel and Greg each had their favorites and sometimes the choice between two equally wonderful options came down to a round of rock, paper, scissors.

They spent their mornings on the cookbook, then moved to the restaurant. There the heated discussions continued as they prepped for the evening's dinner service. Somehow Ana Raquel found herself getting more and more involved with the cooking.

Once the last patron left, she and Greg returned their attention to the cookbook. They worked late into the night to find the right combination of savory and sweet, entrees, appetizers and desserts. They'd agreed on easy recipes, filled with flavor. The kind of food you could serve your family and the boss when he or she came over.

Through a friend of Greg's, they'd made contact with a publisher and quickly found themselves dealing with a deadline. But the book was finally finished.

The best part of the project had been working with Greg. He was exactly who he seemed to be—a nice man she could depend on. He could be stubborn, but never aggressive. He was reasonable, if quirky. And lately, when he smiled, she felt her world get a little brighter.

Ana Raquel chopped furiously. The key to a successful service was prep work, she reminded herself. Tonight was a special dinner at Café. Advance copies of the cookbook had arrived. She and Greg would be handing them out at the end of the dinner where every item on the menu was based on the *Fool's Gold Cookbook*.

Life-Changing Guacamole was offered alongside Bubbly Feta and Sweet Pepper Dip with Pita Crisps. There were entrees for every taste and a dessert buffet that ranged from S'Mores Bars to Triple-Chocolate Caramel Party Cake.

She finished chopping the onions and went to work on the garlic. Greg was lining up the proteins they would be using. Music blared from speakers built into the ceiling.

The staff at the restaurant worked well together, she thought, smashing her knife against cloves of garlic, then peeling away the skin. Their movements were practiced, the results tangible in the smoothness of a sauce or the tang of a salad dressing.

Over the past couple of months, she'd found that she enjoyed working with Greg in his kitchen. They argued a lot, but only about what mattered and she won as often as not. Mayor Marsha had been right, she admitted reluctantly. She never would have been able to handle the cookbook on her own.

"OMG!" Linda, one of the hostesses, said, setting a spoon in the sink. "That dressing. It's heavenly."

Greg looked at her. "It's good."

"I want to be buried with it." Linda paused. "Okay, that sounds more gross than I meant."

Ana Raquel chuckled as she finely chopped garlic. A lot of kitchens were filled with tension and competition. She'd had more than her share of that while she'd been in San Francisco. But things were different here. More relaxed.

"Take a break," Greg said, coming up to her station. "I need you to see something."

She set down her knife and followed him to the dining room. Once there, her breath caught in her throat.

Extra tables had been brought in to satisfy the demand for their special tasting dinner. The tablecloths and fresh flowers coordinated with the colors of the book cover. Speaking of the book, there were stacks on a table off to the side. She and Greg would be signing them later.

On the other side of the room, the dessert buffet was already in place. Delectable smells filled the room.

"Dellina did a great job," Ana Raquel murmured.

"It's impressive. I wish my place looked like this all the time."

She turned to him. "It could. Talk to Dellina. She's great with decorating and parties. She has a real eye for how to put rooms together so that people feel relaxed and enjoy themselves."

He smiled at her. "I'll have to do that. I don't have a lot of spare time. The restaurant keeps me busy."

"I can see that." He was getting by with minimal staff. But he was also in that awkward stage—successful, but not making enough to hire everyone he needed. Any extra bodies he could afford were generally serving staff. "You're doing too much yourself. You need help."

"Good help is hard to find."

She shook her head. "You won't have a problem. You're surprisingly easy to work with."

"So are you." He moved toward her. "I'd like you to think about working here. With me. Officially."

Warmth flooded her. To be honest, she'd been thinking about it herself. "I like the Café," she admitted. "The rest of the staff, what you're doing with the menu. It's tempting."

"But?"

"I have my trailer and I love that. Committing to a kitchen is a big deal."

"I'm not asking you to give up your street food," he told her. "I could help with that. We could use it to promote the restaurant and vice versa. We're a good team. Or are you still mad about my beating you for student council president?"

He was teasing, of course, but there was something serious in his eyes. An emotion she couldn't quite fathom.

"I'm not mad," she said, her gaze slipping to his mouth. He hadn't kissed her since that one time when she'd kissed him. She wasn't sure why not. Was she misreading the situation? Did he only want them to be business associates? Because while she wanted that, too, somewhere along the way she might have, possibly, fallen for him.

"Good," he said, wrapping his arm around her. "All right. We have a dinner to prepare. Only our friends and family and California's longest-serving mayor."

The moment was lost, she realized. Or maybe it had never been there at all. Maybe she was the only one thinking there could be more between them.

"As long as there's no pressure," she said, determined to sound upbeat and cheerful. First the dinner tonight. In the morning she would figure out the state of her heart and decide what to do about it.

Chapter 11 begins on page 212

Comfort Food

Homemade Hot Cocoa

This cocoa mix makes a sweet holiday gift. Seal the powder in a clear bag and present it in a colorful mug along with mixing instructions.

Makes 3 cups

- 1½ cups nonfat dry milk
- 1 cup powdered sugar
- ¾ cup unsweetened cocoa powder
- ½ cup white chocolate chips
- 1 tablespoon instant espresso powder
- Pinch of salt
- Hot milk, as needed

TIP: If kept tightly covered, this mix should keep for months.

1. In a food processor, pulse the first 6 ingredients until a powder forms. Pour into a container that can be sealed.
2. For each serving, spoon ⅓ cup cocoa mixture into 1 cup hot milk.

Cheesy Bread Blossom

Dip and bread all in one fun dish. Experiment with different breads and dips. To try: pumpernickel bread and spinach dip, whole-grain bread and artichoke dip. Just make sure it's a dense loaf of bread so it can hold up to the slicing, and a dip that would taste good warm.

- 1 loaf dense bakery bread, unsliced
- ½ cup (1 stick) unsalted butter, melted, plus additional for greasing foil
- ½ cup dip of your choice
- 1 cup sharp cheddar cheese shredded
- ¼ cup fresh chives, chopped

TIP: Baking time will depend on the size of your loaf and the type of dip you use.

1. Preheat oven to 350°F.
2. Using a serrated knife, slice bread lengthwise and then widthwise, cutting almost to the bottom, but not all the way through.
3. Drizzle melted butter into the crevices of the sliced bread. Stuff dip into the crevices. Sprinkle cheese, stuffing to fill each crevice. Sprinkle chives on top.
4. Lightly grease a large square of foil. Loosely wrap bread in prepared foil; place on a baking sheet and bake 15 minutes. Remove foil; bake uncovered an additional 10 minutes.

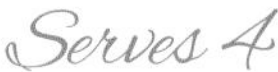

Diner Meatball Hoagies

Meatballs are usually made for pasta sauces, but sandwiching them with melted cheese and warm marinara sauce is so much more fun!

Serves 4

Nonstick cooking spray
1 pound sweet sausage, removed from casing and crumbled
½ cup bread crumbs
1 large egg
⅓ cup ricotta cheese
Salt and black pepper
1 cup prepared marinara sauce
4 hoagie or Italian sandwich rolls, halved
1 cup shredded provolone or mozzarella cheese

TIP: To start the meatballs cooking on a hot surface helps ensure a nicely browned crust. But be careful—the sheet will be hot!

1. Preheat oven to 450°F. Lightly coat a wire rack with nonstick cooking spray; place inside a large-rimmed baking sheet. Place baking sheet in the oven while it warms.
2. In a large bowl, combine sausage, bread crumbs, egg and ricotta until combined. Season with generous amounts of salt and pepper. Using your hands, form mixture into 2-inch balls. You should have about 16 meatballs. Carefully transfer the meatballs to the hot rack on the sheet. Bake 20 minutes, until cooked through. Meanwhile, warm marinara sauce in the microwave or a small saucepan and toast rolls.
3. Layer meatballs, cheese and sauce on the bottom of each warmed roll. Sandwich with the top of the roll.

Oven-Baked Chimichangas

Don't be put off by the number of ingredients—
the recipe is a cinch to put together.

Serves 8

Butter, to grease pan

2 cups cooked chicken, from a rotisserie chicken, shredded

1 can (6 ounces) green chilies, in desired spiciness, drained and chopped

1 cup Monterey Jack or cheddar cheese, shredded

1 tablespoon olive oil, plus additional for brushing tortillas

1 small onion, chopped

1 clove garlic, minced

1 jalapeño pepper, seeded and minced

1 can (16 ounces) refried beans

1 tablespoon chili powder

1 teaspoon ground cumin

2 large tomatoes (or 3 canned, whole, peeled plum tomatoes), chopped

¼ cup fresh cilantro, chopped

Salt and black pepper

8 flour tortillas, burrito-size

Garnishes

Salsa

Sour cream

Guacamole

1. Preheat oven to 400°F. Lightly grease a 9-by-13-inch baking pan. In a large bowl, combine chicken, chilies and cheese.
2. Warm oil in a large skillet over medium heat. Add onions, garlic and jalapeños; cook 4 minutes, until softened, stirring. Stir in refried beans, chili powder, cumin and tomatoes and cook 1 minute, to warm through and combine flavors. Remove from heat; stir in cilantro. Season to taste with salt and pepper.
3. Fill each tortilla with a spoonful of bean mixture and a spoonful of chicken mixture. Fold up two opposite edges, then the other two edges to make an envelope. Place, seam-side down, in the prepared pan. Brush with oil. Bake 20 minutes, until golden and crisp. Serve with desired toppings.

TIP: Don't like it spicy? Omit the canned chilies and jalapeños.

Ethan's Favorite Macaroni and Cheese with Toasted Garlic Bread Crumbs

Foolproof and always a crowd pleaser,
this recipe is sure to become a family favorite.

Serves 8

- 6 tablespoons unsalted butter, divided
- 1 clove garlic, minced
- ½ cup bread crumbs
- 8–10 ounces macaroni or penne pasta
- ¼ cup all-purpose flour
- 2½ cups whole milk
- ¼ teaspoon ground nutmeg
- Salt and black pepper
- 2 cups cheddar cheese, shredded
- 1 cup Monterey Jack cheese, shredded
- ½ cup Parmesan cheese, grated

TIP: If you are making this casserole just before serving, and sauce and pasta are both still hot, you don't need to bake it. Just place it under a hot broiler until golden brown.

1. Melt 2 tablespoons of the butter in a medium nonstick skillet over low heat. Add garlic; cook 30 seconds, stirring constantly. Add bread crumbs; cook 1 minute, until toasted. Scrape into a small bowl.
2. Cook pasta for 2 minutes less than package directions. Drain; rinse with cold water.
3. Preheat oven to 350°F. Melt remaining 4 tablespoons butter in a medium saucepan over medium heat. Sprinkle in flour and stir until a paste forms and flour is completely incorporated. Slowly add milk, a little at a time, stirring constantly and letting the liquid incorporate before adding more milk. Cook for 8 minutes, stirring often, until mixture bubbles and thickens. Stir in nutmeg, salt, pepper, 1½ cups of the cheddar, and the Monterey Jack cheese until melted and blended. Stir in pasta until combined. Spoon mixture into a 3-quart casserole.
4. Sprinkle the top of the casserole with the remaining ½ cup cheddar and Parmesan cheese. Cover evenly with bread-crumb mixture. Bake 30 minutes, until bubbling and warmed through. Let sit 5 minutes before serving.

Lillie's Lasagna Night Special with a Bonus

Red sauce

- 3 tablespoons olive oil
- 1 medium onion, chopped
- 2 stalks celery, thinly sliced
- 4 cloves garlic, chopped
- Salt and black pepper
- 2½ pounds ground chuck
- 2 cans (6 ounce-size) tomato paste
- 2 cups red wine
- 1 can (14¾ ounces) reduced-sodium beef broth
- 1 bay leaf
- 1 tablespoon fresh oregano, chopped, or 1 teaspoon dried

Pasta and white sauce

- 12 lasagna noodles
- ½ cup (1 stick) unsalted butter
- ½ cup all-purpose flour
- 3½ cups whole milk
- Salt and black pepper
- 2½ cups Parmesan cheese, grated

TIP: Extra red sauce will keep for 2 months in the freezer—or in your fridge for a few days. Perfect for a homey Spaghetti Bolognese.

Homemade lasagna takes a bit of time and organization. This recipe rewards your work with a delicious dinner for tonight and an extra amount of sauce to use another night as a pasta topping.

Serves 12–14

For red sauce:

1. Warm oil in a medium saucepan or Dutch oven over medium heat. Add onions, celery and garlic. Season with salt and pepper and cook 10 minutes, until softened and lightly browned, stirring. Add beef, stirring and breaking up meat with a wooden spoon. Cook 15 minutes, until browned. Add tomato paste; cook 4 minutes, stirring to blend. Add wine, stirring to scrape up browned bits from the bottom of the pan. Add broth and enough water to reach 1 inch above meat. Add bay leaf and oregano. Bring to a simmer; cook 3 hours, stirring occasionally and adding water if mixture seems too dry. (You may end up adding several cups of water.)
2. Meanwhile, cook lasagna noodles 2 minutes less than package directions. Drain and rinse under cool water, using your fingers to separate noodles. Set aside 3 cups of the sauce for the lasagna. Reserve the remaining sauce for another night. Discard bay leaf.

For white sauce:

1. Melt butter in a medium saucepan over medium heat. Sprinkle in flour and stir until a paste forms and the flour is completely incorporated. Slowly add milk, a little at a time, stirring constantly and letting the liquid get completely absorbed before adding more milk. Cook for 8 minutes, stirring often, until mixture bubbles and thickens. Season with salt and pepper.
2. Preheat oven to 400°F. Drizzle about ¼ cup of the white sauce in a 9-by-13-inch baking pan. Lay 3 noodles in the bottom of the dish. Cover with 1 cup of red sauce, then ⅓ of remaining white sauce and ⅓ cup Parmesan. Top with 3 more noodles, ⅓ of white sauce and ⅓ cup Parmesan. Top with 3 more noodles, 1 cup red sauce, remaining white sauce and another ⅓ cup Parmesan. Top with 3 remaining noodles and remaining 1 cup red sauce. Sprinkle with remaining 1½ cups Parmesan. Cover lasagna with foil and bake for 35 to 45 minutes, until sauce is bubbly and cheese golden.

Liz's Spaghetti for the Girls

Here's the perfect use for those over-the-hill, must-use-today tomatoes. Any variety, any size.

Serves 4–6

- 4 pounds ripe tomatoes
- ¼ cup olive oil
- 1 small onion, chopped
- 1 small carrot, sliced
- ½ stalk celery, chopped
- 5 cloves garlic, chopped
- Salt and black pepper
- ½ cup red wine
- 1 pound spaghetti

Garnishes

- ½ cup Parmesan cheese, grated
- Fresh basil leaves, sliced

TIP: Use any red wine you have on hand—preferably one you can serve with the finished dish.

1. Set a colander over a bowl. Cut tomatoes in half; squeeze halves over strainer to catch the seeds. Retain the juices in the bowl. Coarsely chop tomato halves.
2. Warm oil in a large saucepan over medium heat. Add onions, carrots, celery and garlic; season with salt and pepper and cook 8 minutes, stirring occasionally. Add wine; cook 2 minutes, until alcohol cooks off. Add chopped tomatoes; bring to a simmer. Reduce heat and simmer 45 minutes, mashing tomatoes with a spoon occasionally. Add reserved tomato juice during cooking if mixture seems dry.
3. Cook pasta according to package directions. In large serving bowl, toss pasta with sauce. Garnish with cheese and basil.

Creamed Spinach and Spiced Chickpea Stir-fry with Coconut Rice

Remember, the spinach will look like a lot when you first put it into the pan—but it will cook down.

Rice

- 1 cup reduced-sodium chicken broth
- 1 cup white rice
- 1 cup unsweetened coconut milk
- Pinch of salt

Stir-fry

- 1 tablespoon olive oil
- 1 can (15 ounces) chickpeas, drained
- 2 cloves garlic, minced
- 1 teaspoon ground cumin
- ½ teaspoon ground ginger
- ½ teaspoon ground coriander
- ¼ teaspoon ground cinnamon
- 12 ounces baby spinach, coarsely chopped
- ¾ cup lowfat buttermilk
- Salt and black pepper

Garnishes

- ¼ cup feta cheese, crumbled
- ¼ cup cashews, chopped

TIP: Buttermilk gives this dish its creamy texture—the recipe won't work as well with skim milk.

1. In a medium saucepan over medium-high heat, bring broth and rice to a simmer. Reduce heat to very low; stir in coconut milk and salt. Cover and cook 17 minutes, without stirring, until liquid has evaporated and rice is just tender.
2. Warm oil in a large, nonstick skillet over medium-low heat. Add chickpeas, garlic, cumin, ginger, coriander and cinnamon; cook 1 minute, stirring. Add spinach; cover and let sit 30 seconds. Uncover; stir-fry 5 minutes, until wilted.
3. Stir in buttermilk and cook until most of the liquid evaporates, yet mixture is still saucy. Season to taste with salt and pepper. Remove from heat; garnish with feta and cashews. Serve with warm rice.

Golden Squash Risotto with Goat Cheese

Risotto has a bad reputation: You must stir the rice constantly, you can only use Arborio rice, and so on. Here we debunk those myths. California medium-grain rice is a perfect stand-in for Arborio and you don't have to stir it the whole time. Just keep an eye on it and stir frequently.

- 2 tablespoons unsalted butter, divided
- 1 medium butternut squash, peeled, seeded and cut into ½-inch cubes
- Salt and black pepper
- 1 small onion, diced
- 2 ounces ham or 1 strip bacon, diced
- 1 cup California medium-grain or Arborio rice
- ½ cup white wine
- 1 can (14¾ ounces) reduced-sodium chicken broth
- 4 cups water
- 1 teaspoon fresh thyme, chopped
- 1 cup (about 4 ounces) goat cheese, crumbled

TIP: For a more traditional risotto, substitute Parmesan for goat cheese.

1. Melt 1 tablespoon of the butter in a large nonstick saucepan over medium-high heat. Add squash; season with salt and pepper and cook 8 minutes, until lightly golden and almost tender. Scrape into a bowl and set aside.
2. Place pan (no need to clean) over medium heat. Melt remaining tablespoon butter. Add onions and ham; cook 4 minutes, stirring. Add rice; cook 1 minute, stirring to coat grains. Stir in wine and cook a few minutes, until wine evaporates, stirring often.
3. Meanwhile, warm broth and 4 cups water in a small covered saucepan over medium-low heat. Leave pot simmering over low heat.
4. Add about ½ cup of the simmering broth to the pot of rice, stirring until liquid evaporates. Keep adding the broth, ½ cup at a time, stirring each time until liquid evaporates. The stirring should be frequent but need not be constant. Cook until rice is cooked through, but still with some bite, about 28 minutes total. Stir in the squash cubes and thyme and cook a few more minutes until squash is tender and warmed through. Remove from heat; stir in goat cheese.

Simple Roast Chicken with Smashed Potatoes

A perfect roast chicken, every time.

Serves 4–6

Chicken

- 1 roasting chicken (about 3 pounds), giblets removed
- Salt and black pepper
- 1 bunch fresh thyme
- 3 tablespoons butter, melted

Potatoes

- 5 medium Yukon Gold potatoes (about 1¾ pounds)
- ½ cup (1 stick) unsalted butter, at room temperature
- ½ cup half-and-half or whole milk, warmed
- 2 scallions, thinly sliced
- Salt and black pepper

TIP: The potatoes and chicken cook in the oven at the same time, but the timing is different for each. It's helpful to have a timer that allows you to enter two different times.

1. Preheat oven to 375°F. Place a rack in a large, shallow roasting pan.
2. Season the chicken cavity with salt and pepper; stuff with thyme. Brush the outside of the chicken with melted butter; season liberally with salt and pepper. Place on the rack in the pan, one wing side up. Place in oven; roast 20 minutes. At this time, add potatoes directly onto the oven rack so that they roast for 50 to 60 minutes, until a knife inserted in one is tender but still meets with just a bit of resistance.
3. Remove the chicken roasting pan from the oven; rotate chicken so that the other wing side is up. Roast 20 minutes. Remove from oven; rotate chicken so that the breast is up. Roast 20 minutes, until an instant-read thermometer inserted in the thickest part of the thigh registers 160°F. Transfer chicken to a cutting board; let it rest 20 minutes.
4. When potatoes are tender, transfer them to a cutting board. Coarsely chop them a few times. Transfer them to a large bowl and smash once with a potato masher. Add butter and milk; smash several more times, until they reach the desired chunkiness. Using a wooden spoon, stir in sliced scallions, salt and pepper, smashing and stirring to combine flavors. Leave potatoes chunky. Serve with chicken.

Rosemary Roast Pork Loin

Sometimes the simplest recipes are the best.
This tender roast makes an elegant, yet effortless, main dish.

Serves 6

- 1 boneless pork roast (about 2½ pounds), tied
- Salt and black pepper
- 4 large cloves garlic, minced
- 2 tablespoons fresh rosemary, chopped and divided, plus several fresh rosemary branches for pan
- 4 tablespoons olive oil, divided
- 6 small red onions, peeled

TIP: For a juicy roast, it's important to let the meat rest at least 10 minutes before serving.

1. Preheat oven to 400°F. Pat roast dry with paper towels; season with salt and pepper. In a small bowl, combine garlic, 1 tablespoon of the chopped rosemary and 2 tablespoons of the oil. Spread mixture all over the roast.
2. Warm the remaining 2 tablespoons of oil in a large, heavy, ovenproof skillet (preferably cast iron) over high heat. Add roast, fat-side down; cook until browned, about 3 minutes. Rotate roast ¼ turn and brown about 2 more minutes. Repeat process until roast is well browned. Using tongs, lift roast off pan; slide rosemary sprigs underneath. Set roast, fat-side down, on top of the sprigs.
3. Cut off a slice on the bottom of each onion so it can sit flat. Using a small knife, make 2 vertical cuts about halfway down through each onion. Push the remaining chopped rosemary into the cuts in the onions; sprinkle with salt. Arrange onions around the roast in the pan.
4. Place skillet in the oven; roast 30 minutes. Remove the skillet; using tongs, turn pork fat-side up. Roast 15 to 20 minutes longer, until an instant-read thermometer registers 145°F. Transfer the roast to a cutting board; let rest 10 minutes. Thinly slice; serve with onions.

Pan-Seared Filet Mignon with Wild Mushroom Ragout

There's no need to gussy up a beautiful piece of meat—salt and plenty of pepper are the only garnishes needed. Shiitake and cremini mushrooms work well in this savory sauce, but feel free to use any mushroom.

Serves 4

Filet

- 4 filets mignon (5 ounces each, about 1½ inches thick)
- Salt and black pepper
- 1 tablespoon olive oil

Ragout

- 1 tablespoon olive oil
- 1 tablespoon unsalted butter
- 1 pound wild mushrooms, stemmed and thickly sliced
- 3 shallots, very thinly sliced
- 1 tablespoon fresh thyme leaves or 1 teaspoon dried thyme
- Salt and black pepper
- ½ cup reduced-sodium chicken broth
- 2 tablespoons red-wine vinegar

TIP: Use large-grained sea salt and freshly ground pepper to season the steak. Sea salt adds an intense flavor to most savory dishes, but should not be used in baking, since it doesn't dissolve the way table salt does.

For filet:

1. Pat filets dry with a paper towel; season generously with salt and pepper. Warm oil in a large, heavy skillet (preferably cast iron) over medium-high heat. Cook steaks 5 minutes per side for medium-rare, or to desired doneness. Transfer to a serving platter and cover to keep warm.

For ragout:

1. Warm olive oil and butter in the same skillet (no need to clean) over medium heat. Add mushrooms; cook 6 minutes, until lightly brown, stirring often. Add shallots, thyme, salt and pepper, and cook 4 minutes, stirring, until mushrooms give off their liquid and are tender. Add broth and vinegar and cook until the ragout is reduced to the consistency of a sauce. Pour sauce over filets on the platter.

Pan-Fried Chicken Breasts with Crisp Rosemary Roast Potatoes

Plain chicken breasts become family-pleasing when pan-fried with a golden crust and served with crisp potatoes.

Potatoes

2 pounds Yukon Gold Potatoes, cut into ½-inch-thick slices

1 tablespoon salt

4 tablespoons olive oil

2 tablespoons fresh rosemary, chopped

Chicken

4 boneless, skinless chicken breast halves (about 1¾ pounds), tenders removed and reserved for another use

2 large eggs, beaten

1 cup bread crumbs

Salt and black pepper

3 tablespoons olive oil

TIP: You may need to add oil as the chicken is cooking.

For potatoes:

1. Preheat oven to 400°F; place oven rack in lowest position and a large-rimmed baking sheet on rack to warm. Place potatoes and salt in a medium saucepan; add water to cover by 1 inch. Bring to a boil over high heat. Reduce heat; simmer 5 minutes, until slightly softened but not cooked through. Drain potatoes; transfer to a large bowl. Toss potatoes with 4 tablespoons oil and rosemary; spread on a warmed baking sheet. Roast 20 minutes, until crisp. Using tongs, flip potatoes. Roast 10 to 15 minutes, until crisp and cooked through.

For chicken:

1. Meanwhile, pound chicken breasts into ⅓-inch thickness. Set up two shallow bowls, one with beaten eggs and one with a mixture of bread crumbs, salt and pepper.
2. Warm 3 tablespoons oil in a large heavy skillet over high heat. Dip chicken in egg, then in bread crumbs, turning to coat both sides. Place chicken in the hot pan and cook 5 minutes per side, until golden brown and cooked through.

Seared Pecan Salmon with Warm Lentils

Pecan-crusted salmon, paired with Dijon-flavored lentils, makes a meal that's fancy enough for company yet simple enough for a weeknight.

- 3½ cups water, plus more if needed
- ¾ cup dried lentils (preferably small lentils de puy)
- 1 large garlic clove, chopped
- Salt and black pepper
- 2 tablespoons red-wine vinegar
- ½ teaspoon Dijon mustard
- 2 tablespoons olive oil, divided
- 1 cup cherry tomatoes, halved
- ¼ cup fresh dill leaves, chopped
- 4 salmon fillets (about 5 ounces each)
- ¼ cup pecans, finely chopped

TIP: Depending on the heat of your flame, you may find that all the liquid cooks off at the end of the lentil cooking time. Keep an eye on the lentils as they cook and add water if it's needed.

1. Combine 3½ cups water, lentils, garlic, salt and pepper in a medium saucepan over high heat. Bring to a boil; reduce heat and simmer 18 minutes, until lentils are just tender. Drain; transfer to a bowl. Stir in vinegar, mustard and 1 tablespoon of the oil. Fold in tomatoes and dill.
2. Warm remaining 1 tablespoon oil in a large nonstick skillet over medium-high heat. Season salmon with salt and pepper. Press pecans into nonskinned side of fillets to coat.
3. Add salmon, skin-side down, to hot pan. Cook 5 minutes. Turn and cook 5 minutes longer, or until fish feels firm, but not hard to the touch. Serve fillets on top of warm lentils.

Sunday Night Fried Chicken

This foolproof fry-and-bake cooking method cuts down on the amount of fat used and ensures evenly cooked chicken.

- 1¼ cups buttermilk, divided
- 1 teaspoon garlic powder, divided
- 1 teaspoon paprika, divided
- Salt and black pepper
- 1 whole chicken (about 3½ pounds), cut into 8 pieces
- 1¾ cups vegetable oil
- 1½ cups all-purpose flour
- 1 teaspoon baking powder

TIP: The chicken coating will be lumpy—that's what gives you thick, crispy bits after frying.

1. In a large bowl, whisk 1 cup of the buttermilk, ½ teaspoon garlic powder, ½ teaspoon paprika and a generous amount of salt and pepper. Add chicken pieces and turn to coat. Cover bowl and refrigerate 1 hour, or overnight.
2. Preheat oven to 400°F. Warm oil in a large Dutch oven or a deep-side, 12-inch skillet over high heat. Place a wire rack on a large-rimmed baking sheet. In a large bowl, whisk flour, baking powder, remaining garlic powder, remaining paprika and additional salt and pepper. Drizzle in remaining ¼ cup buttermilk; whisk to create small lumps in the flour mixture. Working with one piece of chicken at a time, dredge the chicken in the flour mixture, then place each piece on the rack on the baking sheet.
3. When oil reaches 375°F, or when a piece of flour batter sizzles and browns when dropped in, add chicken in batches. Cook 5 minutes, until golden brown. Using tongs, carefully turn chicken and cook 4 minutes, until golden all over. Transfer to the rack on the baking sheet, place in oven and bake 20 minutes, or until thermometer inserted in breast registers 160°F and in leg or thigh registers 175°F. (Note: Smaller pieces may cook more quickly.)

Classic Frosted Brownie

For moist and fudgy brownies, make sure to remove the pan from the oven when brownies are just set. Better they are slightly gooey in the middle than dry and overbaked.

Makes 32

Brownies

- Butter, to grease pan
- 1¼ cups all-purpose flour
- 1 teaspoon salt
- 1 cup (2 sticks) unsalted butter, cut into 8 chunks
- 11 ounces semisweet chocolate, chips or chopped
- 2 tablespoons unsweetened cocoa powder
- 1 teaspoon instant espresso powder
- 5 large eggs, at room temperature
- 2 cups granulated sugar
- 1 tablespoon pure vanilla extract

Frosting

- 3 ounces unsweetened chocolate, chopped
- ½ cup (1 stick) unsalted butter, room temperature and cut into 8 pieces
- 1¼ cups powdered sugar
- 1 teaspoon pure vanilla extract

TIP: Use the butter wrapper to grease the foil pan liner.

For brownies:

1. Preheat oven to 350°F. Line a 9-by-13-inch baking pan with foil, letting the edges hang over the pan sides. Lightly butter foil.
2. In a medium bowl, whisk flour and salt. In a glass bowl, microwave butter and chocolate until chocolate is melted. Whisk in cocoa and espresso powder.
3. In a large bowl with an electric mixer on high speed, beat eggs and sugar until well blended. Beat in vanilla and melted chocolate mixture until smooth and shiny. Reduce mixer speed to low; beat in dry ingredients just until blended.
4. Scrape batter into prepared pan and smooth the top. Bake 30 minutes, until shiny on top and just set. Transfer pan to a wire rack to cool completely.

For frosting:

1. Melt chocolate in the microwave; stir until smooth. In a bowl with an electric mixer on high speed, beat butter until creamy. Add powdered sugar and vanilla; beat 3 minutes until blended. Spoon in melted chocolate; beat for 1 minute.
2. Using foil edges as handles, lift the entire block of brownies from the pan. Spread frosting onto the cool brownies.

Pumpkin Whoopie Pies

Whoopie pies are a fun dessert for a winter party or a great addition to a bake sale.

Makes about 13 sandwich cookies

Cookies

- 2¾ cups all-purpose flour
- 2 teaspoons cream of tartar
- 1 teaspoon baking soda
- ½ teaspoon salt
- 1 teaspoon pumpkin-pie spice
- 1 teaspoon ground cinnamon
- 1 cup (2 sticks) unsalted butter, at room temperature
- 1½ cups granulated sugar
- 1 large egg
- ¾ cup pumpkin purée (not pumpkin-pie mix)

Topping

- ⅓ cup granulated sugar
- 2 tablespoons ground cinnamon

Filling

- 6 tablespoons cream cheese, at room temperature
- 4 tablespoons (½ stick) unsalted butter, at room temperature
- 1¾–2 cups powdered sugar

Pumpkin Whoopie Pies

Recipe continued from previous page.

For cookies:

1. Line 2 large baking sheets with parchment paper or nonstick baking pads. In a large bowl, whisk flour, cream of tartar, baking soda, salt, pumpkin-pie spice and cinnamon.
2. In a large bowl with an electric mixer, cream butter and 1½ cups sugar until light and fluffy. Scrape down the sides of the bowl with a rubber spatula. Beat in egg and pumpkin purée until combined, about 30 seconds. Reduce speed to low; add the dry ingredients and beat at low speed until just combined. Cover bowl and refrigerate 20 minutes.

TIP: For guaranteed liftoff and ease in cleanup, line your baking sheets with parchment paper or invest in a nonstick baking pad.

For topping:

1. Preheat oven to 375°F. In a small bowl, whisk ⅓ cup sugar and cinnamon.
2. Scoop up about 2 tablespoons of cookie dough; roll between your palms to form a ball. Roll the ball in cinnamon-sugar topping; place on the prepared baking sheet. Repeat with remaining dough, spacing balls about 2 inches apart. Using a glass, press down on the balls to slightly flatten them. Bake 10 minutes, rotating the sheet halfway through baking, or until edges are set and just beginning to brown, but the centers are still soft and puffy. Let cookies cool in the pan for 10 minutes. Cookies will fall slightly. Transfer to a wire rack to cool completely.

For filling:

1. In a large bowl with an electric mixer on high speed, beat cream cheese and butter until blended. Add powdered sugar; beat until light and fluffy. Add additional sugar as needed to reach desired consistency. Sandwich filling between 2 cooled cookies.

White and Dark Chocolate Chunk Cookie Pie

An oversized chocolate chunk cookie shaped like a pie—what fun for kids and adults alike!

- 1¼ cups all-purpose flour
- ½ teaspoon baking soda
- ½ teaspoon salt
- ¼ teaspoon baking powder
- ½ cup (1 stick) unsalted butter
- 1 cup light-brown sugar
- 1 large egg, plus 1 egg yolk
- 2 teaspoons pure vanilla extract
- 6 ounces (about 1 cup) semisweet chocolate chunks
- 6 ounces (about 1 cup) white chocolate chunks
- ¾ cup toasted walnuts, chopped

TIP: Substitute a 9-inch cake pan if you don't have the correct size cast-iron skillet. Melt the butter in the microwave and prep the cake pan by rubbing the empty butter wrapper on the bottom and sides.

1. Preheat oven to 350°F. In a bowl, whisk flour, baking soda, salt and baking powder.
2. Melt butter in a 9-inch cast-iron skillet over low heat. Remove from heat; whisk in brown sugar until completely dissolved and smooth.
3. In a medium bowl, whisk egg, yolk and vanilla until frothy. Whisk in melted butter mixture from the pan. Fold in dry ingredients just until blended. Fold in both chocolates and walnuts. Scrape dough back into the buttery skillet. Bake 20 to 25 minutes until just set in the middle and shiny on top. Transfer to a wire rack to cool.

Chocolate Marble Gooey Bars

Crazy easy, crazy delicious. Almost magically, the cake mix forms a shortbreadlike crust for the marbled cream-cheese filling.

Crust

- Butter, to grease pan
- 1 box yellow cake mix
- ½ cup (1 stick) unsalted butter, melted
- 1 large egg

Filling

- 1 package (8 ounces) cream cheese, at room temperature
- 2 large eggs
- 1 teaspoon pure vanilla extract
- 1 box (1 pound) powdered sugar
- ½ cup (1 stick) unsalted butter, at room temperature
- ⅔ cup semisweet chocolate chips
- Powdered sugar, for sprinkling

TIP: Don't be afraid to remove bars from the oven when the filling still looks underbaked.

For crust:

1. Preheat oven to 350°F. Lightly butter a 9-by-13-inch baking pan.
2. With an electric mixer at high speed, beat cake mix, melted butter and egg until blended. Dough will be a thick mass. Press mixture evenly into prepared pan.

For filling:

1. In the same electric mixer bowl, beat cream cheese until smooth. Add eggs and vanilla; beat until blended. Beat in powdered sugar. Reduce mixer speed; beat in butter.
2. In a microwaveable bowl, melt chocolate chips in the microwave. Using a measuring cup, scoop out ⅔ cup of filling batter; stir into melted chocolate until blended. Spread the remaining filling over the cake layer. Drop chocolate batter in blobs over the filling. Using a knife, swirl the batter to create a marbled effect in the filling. Bake for 35 minutes, until golden brown around the edges but still jiggly in the center. Transfer to a wire rack to cool. When cool, cut into bars and sprinkle with powdered sugar.

Chunky Chewy Oatmeal Toffee Cookies

The trick to baking a really thick, chewy cookie is to chill the dough before baking. You can form and bake the cookies when the dough is cold.

Makes about 18

- 1 cup all-purpose flour
- ½ teaspoon baking soda
- ¼ teaspoon salt
- ½ cup (1 stick) unsalted butter, at room temperature
- ¾ cup light-brown sugar, packed
- 1 large egg
- 1 teaspoon pure vanilla extract
- 1¼ cups rolled oats
- 1 cup chopped chocolate-covered toffee bars (such as Heath bars)
- 1 cup walnuts or pecans, chopped

TIP: Traditional (or "old-fashioned") rolled oats, not the quick-cooking kind, work best for baking.

1. Preheat oven to 350°F. Line 2 baking sheets with parchment paper or nonstick baking pads. In a medium bowl, whisk flour, baking soda and salt.
2. In a large bowl with an electric mixer on high speed, beat butter, brown sugar, egg and vanilla until blended. Add dry ingredients; beat just until combined. Remove from mixer; fold in oats, toffee and walnuts. Chill the dough for at least 20 minutes or up to 24 hours.
3. Drop cookies in large craggy spoonfuls onto the prepared baking sheets. Bake 10 minutes, until golden around the edges but still wet-looking in the middle. Let cool in the pans for 5 minutes, then transfer to a wire rack to cool completely.

CHAPTER 11

The evening passed in a whirlwind of activity. The guests came in waves, filling tables, then lingering as others arrived. It was like regular dinner service on steroids. The kitchen was controlled insanity, with everyone working together to keep food moving.

Somewhere around ten, Linda came and got Ana Raquel and Greg. They walked out into the front of the restaurant only to find nearly everyone they knew in town crowding into the room. Ana Raquel's sisters were there, as were Greg's extended family. The mayor, of course, the city council, other small business owners and friends. Lots and lots of friends.

She and Greg were given a standing ovation. People called out, "Wonderful meal" and "Come cook at my house!" She laughed even as she felt tears burning in her eyes.

Greg led her over to the table with the books and they sat down next to each other to begin signing.

Ana Raquel signed until her fingers cramped, then kept on going. Sometime after midnight, the last of their guests left. The kitchen staff had already cleaned up, leaving the counters gleaming and bare and a couple of small pots simmering on the stove. As she inhaled the scent of their dinner, her stomach growled.

Greg flashed her a grin. "Me, too. Starving. I'm not sure I've eaten since breakfast."

"I know I haven't."

She went to get the plates. When she returned to the stove, he was still there, but now he held a bottle of champagne.

"I thought we deserved a toast for all we've been through."

"I agree."

He opened the bottle and poured them each a glass. They raised their glasses to each other.

"To the *Fool's Gold Cookbook,*" he said.

"The cookbook."

They touched glasses, then sipped. The liquid was sweet and bubbly, tickling her nose and making her laugh. She carried the bottle to the small table in the back of the kitchen while Greg served their meals.

She was tired, she thought, but happy. She was still confused about her feelings for Greg and not sure what to do about his job offer. While she liked working with him, she wasn't sure she could separate her personal feelings from her professional duties. She didn't want to be one of those women mooning over her business partner. That was just plain sad and kind of embarrassing. She wanted better for herself.

Of course, a case could be made that thinking she might want more and not asking for it was stupid. Maybe he felt the same way. Maybe he'd secretly been in love with her for years.

That last thought made her chuckle. How preposterous, she thought.

He walked to the table, a plate in each hand. "What's so funny?"

"Nothing. I'm so tired, I'm getting punchy. I'm only having one glass of champagne so I don't fall asleep in my soup."

He set down the food. She waited for him to take a seat, but instead he moved closer and cupped her face in his hands.

"Ana Raquel," he murmured, right before he kissed her.

Chapter 12 begins on page 242

Holidays

Bacon-Roasted Brussels Sprouts

Braising Brussels sprouts in the oven makes for tender, not soggy, sprouts.

4 strips bacon

2 tablespoons unsalted butter

2 pounds Brussels sprouts, trimmed and halved if large

1 medium shallot, chopped

1 cup reduced-sodium chicken broth

Salt and black pepper

TIP: To trim sprouts, slice off tough stems and remove any loose outer leaves. Cut any large sprouts in half.

1. Preheat oven to 400°F. Cook bacon in a large, ovenproof skillet until crisp. Transfer bacon to a paper towel–lined plate; crumble. Pour off and discard all but 2 tablespoons of the drippings from the pan. Add butter to the pan with the drippings; warm until melted, still over medium heat. Add sprouts and shallots; cook 8 minutes, until sprouts are lightly golden, stirring often.
2. Pour broth into the pan; broth should come about ⅓ of the way up the side of the sprouts. Bring to a simmer over medium-high heat. Transfer pan to the oven; cook 13 to 15 minutes, until sprouts are just tender and bright green.
3. Using a slotted spoon, transfer roasted sprouts to a large serving bowl. Toss with crumbled bacon. Season to taste with salt and pepper. Discard any broth remaining in pan.

Chicken Teriyaki Skewers

These savory bites make a hearty appetizer or a fun addition to a buffet table.

Serves 4–6

- ⅔ cup low-sodium soy sauce
- ¼ cup light-brown sugar
- 2 tablespoons fresh ginger, peeled and finely minced
- 2 cloves garlic, minced
- 2 teaspoons sesame or vegetable oil
- 1 teaspoon cornstarch
- 2 pounds chicken tenders (about 16)
- Nonstick cooking spray

TIP: The size and weight of packaged chicken tenders vary greatly. The cooking time and resulting number of skewers depend on the size of the tenders used.

1. In a large resealable plastic bag, combine the first 6 ingredients until blended. Add chicken; turn bag to coat. Refrigerate and let the chicken marinate at least 30 minutes or up to 24 hours. Turn the bag a few times while marinating.
2. If you're using wooden skewers, soak them in water at least 30 minutes before cooking to prevent them from scorching. Lightly coat a rimmed baking sheet with nonstick cooking spray.
3. Preheat broiler. Remove chicken from the marinade, setting aside the marinade. Slide 1 tender on each skewer lengthwise, threading so the tenders are securely attached. Place the skewers on the prepared baking sheet and broil about 4 minutes, until chicken is cooked through and golden brown, turning once.
4. Pour reserved marinade into a small pan and bring it to a boil over high heat. Reduce heat to medium; let the marinade simmer 4 minutes, until it's reduced and slightly syrupy. Pour the marinade into a small bowl for drizzling over skewers.

Retro Stuffed Mushrooms

Stuffed mushroom caps are a classic party hors d'oeuvre.
Serve them with a green salad for a light dinner.

Makes about 12

- 12 large button or cremini mushrooms
- 2 tablespoons unsalted butter, plus additional for greasing baking sheet
- 2 tablespoons minced onions
- 1 clove garlic, minced
- 2 tablespoons bread crumbs
- 2 tablespoons Parmesan cheese, grated
- Salt and black pepper

TIP: You can use plain or seasoned bread crumbs.

1. Preheat oven to 400°F. Twist off the stem of each mushroom; finely chop the stems. Place caps, cavity-side up, on a lightly greased baking sheet.
2. Melt butter in a small skillet over medium-low heat. Add chopped mushroom stems, onions and garlic; cook 4 minutes, stirring often. Remove from heat, stir in bread crumbs. Stuff caps with mixture. Sprinkle with cheese; season with salt and pepper. Bake 18 to 20 minutes, until mushrooms are softened and warmed through.

Parmesan-Dusted Kale Chips

These addictive salty snacks are a lighter and certainly more nutritious alternative to chips and dip before a holiday feast.

Serves 6

- 1 bunch kale, any variety
- 1 tablespoon olive oil
- Salt
- 2 tablespoons Parmesan cheese, finely grated

TIP: Kale chips are very delicate and won't hold up to a dip, so handle them gently.

1. Preheat oven to 350°F. Line 2 baking sheets with parchment paper. Slice woody stems off each kale stalk. Coarsely chop leaves.
2. In a large bowl, combine chopped kale, oil and salt. Using your hands, toss until kale is well coated. Sprinkle with Parmesan. Spread mixture evenly onto prepared sheets. Bake 12 to 15 minutes, stirring several times and rotating baking sheets once. Chips should be light and crisp but not browned. Transfer sheets to a wire rack to cool. Store chips in a tightly covered container.

Sweet Potato Biscuits

Serve these special-occasion biscuits warm, with butter.

Makes 8

- 2 medium sweet potatoes (about 1½ pounds), pricked all over with a fork
- 1 tablespoon orange juice
- 1½ cups plus 2 tablespoons cake flour
- 3 tablespoons light-brown sugar
- 3 teaspoons baking powder
- ¼ teaspoon baking soda
- ½ teaspoon salt
- 4 tablespoons (½ stick) cold unsalted butter, chopped
- 2 tablespoons shortening, chopped

TIP: The dough will be crumbly at first; try to handle it as little as possible as you work to form the biscuits. If cake flour is unavailable, you can substitute all-purpose flour, keeping in mind that 1 cup cake flour is the equivalent of 1 cup all-purpose flour minus 2 tablespoons.

1. Place pricked sweet potatoes on a plate; microwave 15 minutes, until very soft, turning sweet potatoes a few times during cooking. Remove to a cutting board; slice in half. Scoop flesh into a bowl; add orange juice and mash until smooth. You should have about 1¼ cups. Let cool to room temperature.
2. Preheat oven to 425°F. Line a baking sheet with parchment paper or a nonstick baking pad. In a food processor, pulse flour, brown sugar, baking powder, baking soda, salt, butter and shortening until mixture resembles coarse meal. Add potatoes; pulse until blended.
3. Dump dough out onto a lightly floured surface; knead a few minutes until dough holds together. Form dough into a 1-inch-thick circle. Using a 2-inch biscuit cutter, cut out as many rounds as possible. Transfer rounds to the prepared baking sheet. Gather the remaining dough, form into a 1-inch-thick circle, cut out additional biscuits and place them on the baking sheet. Bake 18 minutes, until golden and just firm. Transfer to a wire rack to cool.

Garlic Green Beans with Toasted Hazelnuts

Every holiday table benefits from a steaming bowl of bright green beans. Especially when they are embellished with crunchy nuts, as these are.

- 2 pounds green beans, trimmed
- 2 tablespoons olive oil
- 2 large cloves garlic, minced
- ½ cup peeled hazelnuts, coarsely chopped
- Salt and black pepper

TIP: If hazelnuts are unavailable, substitute any nut you like.

1. Bring a large pot of salted water to a boil. Add beans and cook 5 minutes, until just tender.
2. Meanwhile, warm oil in a large skillet over medium heat. Add garlic and cook 30 seconds, stirring. Add nuts and cook 2 minutes, until golden, stirring.
3. Drain beans; add to skillet. Season with salt and pepper; toss to coat. Transfer to a serving bowl.

Roasted Beet and Baby Arugula Salad with Champagne Vinaigrette

This salad is full of color and crunch. It's more work than a simple tossed salad, so make it for a special meal. If champagne vinegar is unavailable, use white-wine vinegar instead.

Serves 6–8

Vinaigrette

- 3 tablespoons champagne vinegar
- 1 tablespoon minced shallots
- 1 teaspoon honey
- ¼ cup extra-virgin olive oil
- Salt and black pepper

Salad

- 1½ pounds red beets, trimmed and rinsed
- 6 cups baby arugula leaves
- 2 cups mixed baby salad greens
- ⅓ cup pine nuts, toasted

TIP: Roasting time for beets will depend on their size.

For vinaigrette:

1. In a medium bowl, whisk all dressing ingredients until blended.

For salad:

1. Preheat oven to 400°F. Place beets in a medium ovenproof pan with a lid. Add water to come about ½ inch up sides of the pan. Cover the pan. Roast 1 hour, until fork-tender. Remove and let cool slightly. Peel, quarter and thinly slice beets.
2. In a large serving bowl, toss beets with greens, vinaigrette and pine nuts. Serve immediately.

Lemon and Herb Roasted Turkey

Simple and straightforward.
This recipe is for those who prefer not to stuff the bird.

Serves 10–12

- 1 fresh or frozen thawed turkey (about 14 pounds)
- 2 lemons, halved
- Salt and black pepper
- 1 small bunch fresh rosemary
- 4 tablespoons (½ stick) unsalted butter, at room temperature
- 2 cups reduced-sodium chicken broth, as needed
- 2 carrots, chopped
- 2 stalks celery, chopped
- 1 medium onion, cut into large chunks
- ½ cup dry white wine

TIP: If you have a stuffing you want to use, omit the rosemary branches.

1. Preheat oven to 350°F. Rinse turkey and pat dry. Squeeze two lemon halves into the cavity of the turkey; stuff squeezed halves into the cavity. Season the cavity with salt and pepper. Stuff the cavity with rosemary branches. Squeeze the remaining lemon halves over the turkey; season with salt and pepper. Secure the turkey with skewers or sew shut with a trussing needle. Tuck wings under the back. Tie legs together.
2. Place a wire rack in a large roasting pan. Set turkey on the wire rack, breast side up. Rub the turkey breast with butter. Loosely tent the breast with foil.
3. Pour 1 cup of chicken broth into the pan, then scatter carrots, celery and onions around the turkey in the bottom of the pan. Roast 10 to 12 minutes per pound, until an instant-read thermometer inserted midthigh registers 165°F. Baste several times with pan juices. Remove foil in the last hour of cooking. Using tongs, transfer the turkey to a carving board. Let it rest for 20 minutes.

For gravy:

1. Set a colander atop a large liquid measuring cup. Pour contents of the roasting pan into the colander. Press down on the vegetables in the strainer to extract juices. You should have about 1 cup of juices; add broth to measure 1½ cups. Discard vegetables in colander.
2. Place the roasting pan (no need to clean) over 2 burners set at medium-heat. Stir in wine; cook 2 minutes, scraping the bottom of the pan to release browned bits. Add the strained pan-juice mixture. Bring to a simmer; cook 5 minutes, or until gravy is reduced and thickens slightly, stirring often. Slice turkey and serve with gravy.

Sour Cream Mashed Potatoes

No holiday table is complete without a steaming bowl of creamy mashed potatoes.

Serves 8

- 3 pounds Yukon gold or boiling potatoes, peeled and cut into 1-inch chunks
- ½ cup (1 stick) unsalted butter, chopped
- ¾ cup sour cream
- ⅔ cup whole milk
- Salt and black pepper

TIP: Full-fat sour cream can withstand heat better than reduced-fat versions.

1. Combine potatoes, salt and enough water to cover the potatoes by at least 3 inches in a large saucepan. Bring to a boil over high heat; reduce heat and simmer 20 minutes, until a sharp knife inserted in a potato slides out very easily. Drain; return potatoes to the hot empty pot over low heat. Shake pan to evaporate any water left on potatoes.
2. Add butter, sour cream and milk to the pot, still over low heat. Mash until the potatoes reach desired consistency. Season with salt and pepper.

Southwestern Cornbread Sausage Dressing

If your cornbread is extremely fresh,
allow it to dry out a bit before using it.

Serves 8–10

- 2 tablespoons olive oil, plus additional for greasing pan
- 1 pound sweet sausage, removed from casing and crumbled
- 2 yellow onions, diced
- 2 bell peppers, any color, diced
- 2 stalks celery, thinly sliced
- 1 package (10-ounce) frozen corn, thawed
- 2 tablespoons fresh thyme leaves, chopped
- 1 tablespoon ground cumin
- 2 large eggs
- 2 tablespoons maple syrup
- Salt and black pepper
- 1½ pounds store-bought cornbread, cut into small dice or coarsely crumbled (about 10 cups)
- 1 cup reduced-sodium chicken broth
- ½ cup chopped fresh Italian parsley
- Butter, to grease foil

1. Preheat oven to 350°F. Lightly oil a 9-by-13-inch glass or ceramic casserole dish.
2. Warm 1 tablespoon of the oil in a Dutch oven or a large saucepan over medium heat; add sausage and cook about 6 minutes, until browned, stirring often. Using a slotted spoon, remove sausage to a large bowl. Add remaining oil to the drippings in the pan, still over medium heat. Cook onions, peppers and celery 10 minutes, until softened, stirring often. Stir in corn, thyme and cumin; cook 2 minutes, stirring. Remove from heat.
3. In a large bowl, whisk eggs, maple syrup, salt and pepper. Fold in sausage mixture. Gently fold in crumbled cornbread, broth and parsley. Do not overmix.
4. Spoon mixture into the prepared casserole dish, cover tightly with buttered foil. Bake 25 minutes. Uncover; bake 15 minutes more, until golden brown on top and warmed through.

TIP: Although curly and flat-leaf parsley may be used interchangeably, flat-leaf (or Italian, as it's also called) parsley has a more pungent flavor. Dried parsley has no flavor at all.

Honey-Mustard Holiday Ham

A baked ham is perfect party fare.
Serve warm or at room temperature.

Serves 14

- 8 pounds smoked ham with rind
- 2 cups apple cider or apple juice, divided
- ⅔ cup light-brown sugar
- ½ cup Dijon mustard
- ¼ cup honey
- ¼ teaspoon ground cloves

TIP: You want the spicy-sweet sauce to thicken to a glaze before you apply it to the ham. The reducing time will depend on the thickness of your cider.

1. Preheat oven to 325°F. Place ham on a wire rack; set the rack in a roasting pan. Pour 1 cup of the apple cider over the ham. Cover ham completely with parchment paper, then heavy-duty foil, sealing around the edges of the pan. Bake 20 minutes per pound, until an instant-read thermometer inserted in the center of the ham registers 145°F. Remove ham from the oven; increase oven temperature to 375°F.
2. In a small saucepan over medium heat, bring the remaining cider, brown sugar, mustard, honey and cloves to a simmer, stirring. Cook until sugar completely dissolves and sauce thickens.
3. Remove foil and parchment from the roasting pan; drain off any liquid collected in the pan. Using a long, sharp knife, cut off rind and all but a thin layer of fat from ham. Score the remaining ham in a diamond pattern. Using a brush, spread sauce over the ham. Bake 30 minutes, spooning any glaze that slides off the back onto the ham. Transfer to a serving platter; cover and let the ham rest 20 minutes.

Raspberry Linzer Sandwich Cookies

These classic treats make an elegant addition to a dessert buffet or a sweet hostess gift for a holiday gathering. The rolled-out dough can be wrapped airtight and stored in the refrigerator for up to 3 days or in the freezer for up to 2 months. Just thaw the dough enough to cut and go from there.

Makes 18 sandwich cookies

- 1½ cups raw almonds or hazelnuts, whole
- 1½ cups all-purpose flour
- 1 teaspoon ground cinnamon
- ¼ teaspoon ground cloves
- Pinch of salt
- 1 large egg
- ½ cup (1 stick) unsalted butter, at room temperature
- ½ cup granulated sugar
- Powdered sugar, for sprinkling
- Raspberry jam, as needed

TIP: Wait to create jam sandwiches until the day you'll be serving them. Filled cookies will become soggy overnight.

---

1. In the bowl of a food processor, process almonds just until ground. You should have about 1½ cups ground almonds. Add flour, cinnamon, cloves and salt; pulse just until combined. Quickly pulse in egg until blended.
2. In the bowl of an electric mixer, beat butter and sugar until well combined. Add nut mixture just until blended. Don't overmix. Divide dough in half; place each half in between 2 sheets of plastic wrap or wax paper. Flatten into a disk; roll out (still wrapped) to a ¼-inch-thick round. Repeat process with the other half of the dough. Refrigerate both dough slabs, still wrapped and as flat as possible, for 2 hours, until very firm.
3. Preheat oven to 375°F. Line 2 baking sheets with parchment paper or nonstick baking pads. Peel off the top sheet of plastic wrap from one slab of dough and, using a 2-inch scalloped or round cookie cutter, cut out as many cookies as possible. Using one end of a piping tip, cut out a small circle in the center of half the cookies. Using a spatula, transfer cookies to the prepared baking sheets. Gather scraps into a ball; refrigerate until the second slab is rolled out. Repeat the process with the second half of dough. Combine scraps of both dough halves; refrigerate, then roll out and cut as before.
4. Bake cookies, 1 sheet at a time, for 10 to 12 minutes, or until lightly golden around the edges and just firm to the touch. Transfer to a wire rack to cool.
5. Sprinkle cooled cut-out cookies with powdered sugar. Turn the cookies without holes flat-side up; spread with jam. Top with cut-out cookies flat-side down.

Coconut Vanilla Snowball Cupcakes

This big-batch cupcake recipe makes enough for a winter party. The cupcakes look especially pretty on a tiered cake stand.

Makes 24

Cupcakes

- 2½ cups plus 2 tablespoons all-purpose flour
- ¾ teaspoon baking soda
- ½ teaspoon salt
- 12 tablespoons (1½ sticks) unsalted butter, at room temperature
- 1½ cups granulated sugar
- 3 large eggs, at room temperature
- 2 teaspoons pure vanilla extract
- ½ teaspoon pure coconut extract
- ¾ cup sour cream
- 1 cup sweetened flaked coconut

Frosting

- ½ cup (1 stick) unsalted butter, at room temperature
- 2–2½ cups powdered sugar
- 1 teaspoon pure vanilla extract
- Pinch of salt
- 3 tablespoons sour cream
- Sweetened flaked coconut, for garnish

TIP: Eggs blend into cake batter best if they're at room temperature.

1. Preheat oven to 350°F. Line 2 standard 12-cup muffin tins with cupcake liners.
2. In a medium bowl, whisk flour, baking soda and salt until combined.
3. In a large bowl with an electric mixer on high speed, beat butter and sugar until light and fluffy. Add eggs, one at a time, beating well after each addition. Add vanilla and coconut extracts; beat until blended. Reduce mixer speed to low, and alternately add dry ingredients and sour cream, beginning and ending with dry ingredients. Remove from mixer; fold in coconut.
4. Drop batter into cupcake liners, filling each just over halfway full. Bake 18–20 minutes, until golden and set. Let cool in pans for 10 minutes. Transfer to a wire rack to cool completely.
5. For frosting: In a large bowl with an electric mixer on medium-high speed, beat butter until smooth. Add powdered sugar, vanilla and salt; beat until blended and fluffy. Add sour cream; beat just until blended. Fold in additional powdered sugar, if needed.
6. Spread the frosting on cooled cupcakes. Sprinkle a generous amount of coconut over cupcakes.

Chocolate Caramel Pecan Tart

Crust

30 (about 6 ½ ounces) chocolate wafer cookies (such as Nabisco Famous)

Pinch of salt

5 tablespoons unsalted butter, melted

Filling

2 teaspoons instant espresso powder

3 tablespoons hot coffee or water

9 tablespoons unsalted butter, chopped

6 tablespoons heavy cream

3 large eggs, separated

9 ounces semisweet chocolate, chopped

1 teaspoon granulated sugar

Caramel-pecan layer

2 tablespoons heavy cream

8 ounces caramel candies, unwrapped

4 ounces toasted pecans, chopped

Chocolate drizzle

¼ cup heavy cream

⅓ cup chopped semisweet chocolate or chips

TIP: Serve tart at room temperature so the caramel is chewy, not hard.

An elegant tart for a party that (don't tell anyone!) tastes like the most decadent candy bar.

Serves 10

For crust:

1. Preheat oven to 350°F. In the bowl of a food processor, pulse cookies and salt until fine crumbs form. Add butter; pulse just until dough comes together. Dump dough into a 9-inch tart pan with a removable bottom. Using the back of a spoon, press dough evenly in the pan and up the sides. Bake crust for 8 minutes, until slightly puffed and a bit darker in color. Transfer to a wire rack to cool completely.

For filling:

1. In a small bowl, dissolve espresso powder in hot coffee. Melt butter in a small saucepan over medium-low heat. Add dissolved espresso, cream and egg yolks. Warm until mixture measures 160°F on a candy thermometer, stirring constantly. Remove from heat, whisk in chopped chocolate until melted. Pour mixture into a large bowl and let cool to lukewarm.
2. With an electric mixer on high speed, beat egg whites until foamy. Add sugar; beat until stiff peaks form. Fold whites into cooled chocolate mixture until blended. Spoon filling into the cooled crust. Freeze 2 hours, or until firm.

For caramel-pecan layer:

1. Bring a small saucepan of water to a simmer over high heat. Place cream and caramels in a metal bowl; set bowl over simmering water. Cook until caramels are melted, stirring often. Drizzle warm caramel evenly over tart. Immediately sprinkle pecans over caramel so that they stick. Let cool.

For chocolate drizzle:

1. Microwave cream until hot but not boiling. Place chopped chocolate in a bowl; stir in hot cream until blended and of drizzling consistency. Drizzle in a zigzag pattern over the tart. Store tart in refrigerator; let it sit at room temperature until soft enough to cut.

Classic Guinness Gingerbread

Deep, dark, intensely spiced—this is a very special holiday dessert.
More good news—the cake tastes even better the next day.
Wrap cooled cake tightly in plastic and store at room temperature.

Serves 12

Cake

- Butter, for greasing pan
- ¾ cup Guinness or other stout
- 1 teaspoon baking soda
- 1 cup molasses (not blackstrap)
- 1 cup light-brown sugar
- 1 cup granulated sugar
- 3 large eggs
- ¾ cup vegetable oil
- 2 cups all-purpose flour, plus additional for pan
- 1¼ teaspoons baking powder
- 2 tablespoons ground ginger
- 1 teaspoon ground cinnamon
- ¼ teaspoon ground cloves
- Pinch of ground cardamom

Glaze

- 2 tablespoons fresh lemon juice
- 1 cup powdered sugar, sifted
- Zest from 1 lemon

TIP: It's important to generously butter and flour the cake pan to ensure that the cake releases from the pan. The heavier the Bundt pan, the easier it will be to remove the cake from the pan.

For cake:

1. Preheat oven to 350°F. Very generously butter a 9- or 10-inch Bundt pan, making sure to cover every nook and cranny. Dust with flour, knocking out excess.
2. In a small saucepan, bring stout to a simmer over medium-low heat. Remove from heat; stir in baking soda. When foam subsides, stir in molasses and both sugars until dissolved. Scrape mixture into the bowl of an electric mixer. Add eggs and oil; beat until blended.
3. In a large bowl, whisk flour, baking powder, ginger, cinnamon, cloves and cardamom. Slowly add dry ingredients into stout mixture, beating at high speed until completely smooth.
4. Scrape batter into prepared Bundt pan. Tap pan against the counter a few times to release any air bubbles. Bake 50 minutes, until a toothpick comes out with just a few crumbs. Cool in the pan for 10 minutes. Carefully run a metal spatula around the edges of the cake to loosen it from the pan. Turn the cake out onto a wire rack to cool completely.

For glaze:

1. In a medium bowl, whisk lemon juice and powdered sugar until of drizzling consistency. Drizzle glaze over the cake, and sprinkle zest on top of it.

Minty Brownie Bombs

These cookies combine the rich fudginess of brownies with the chewy crunch of cookies. Stuffing them with mint cookie bits and frosting with chocolate mints sends the taste sensation over the top.

Makes about 15

- ½ cup (1 stick) unsalted butter, melted and cooled slightly
- 2 large eggs
- 1 package (18–21 ounces) fudge brownie mix
- 1 cup all-purpose flour
- 1½ cups broken mint chocolate-sandwich cookies (about 13 cookies)
- About 15 mint chocolate wafer candies (such as Andes)

TIP: If mint doesn't appeal to you, use plain chocolate-sandwich cookies (such as Oreos).

1. Preheat oven to 350°F. Line a baking sheet with parchment paper or nonstick liners.
2. In a large bowl, whisk melted butter and eggs until blended. Add brownie mix and flour; stir with a wooden spoon until combined (dough will be thick). Fold in cookie chunks. Drop dough by heaping tablespoon onto prepared sheets. Press down on cookies with your palm to slightly flatten. Bake 8 to 10 minutes, until just set but still a bit undercooked in the middle. While still hot, top each cookie with a mint. Using a spoon, gently push the mint into the cookie, swirling it a bit so it covers most of the cookie. Transfer cookies to a wire rack to cool completely.

Triple-Chocolate Caramel Party Cake

Cake

- Butter, for greasing pans
- 1¾ cups all-purpose flour, plus additional for pan
- 2 cups granulated sugar
- ¾ cup unsweetened cocoa powder
- 2 teaspoons baking soda
- 1 teaspoon baking powder
- 1 teaspoon salt
- 2 large eggs, at room temperature
- ½ cup vegetable oil
- 1 cup buttermilk
- 1 teaspoon pure vanilla extract
- 1 cup warm coffee

Filling and ganache

- 14 ounces semisweet chocolate, chopped or chips
- 14 ounces heavy cream
- 1 cup prepared dulce de leche or thick caramel dip
- About 30 Rolo or other small caramel cup candies, some of them halved

TIP: The longer you allow the ganache to cool, the thicker it will become. You can refrigerate the bowl to speed up cooling, but keep an eye on it to make sure it doesn't become too thick.

Piling chocolate-covered caramels on top of this decadent layer cake makes this a cake fit for a party, any party.

Serves 12

For cake:

1. Preheat oven to 350°F. Butter and flour bottom and sides of two 8-inch cake pans. Line bottoms with parchment paper, then butter and flour the parchment.
2. In a medium bowl, whisk flour, sugar, cocoa, baking soda, baking powder and salt until blended. In a large bowl with an electric mixer on high speed, beat eggs, oil, buttermilk and vanilla. Reduce mixer speed to low; alternately add dry ingredients and coffee just until blended. Batter will be wet.
3. Pour batter into prepared pans. Bake for 35 to 40 minutes, until a toothpick inserted in the center comes out clean. Remove to a wire rack; let cakes cool in the pans for 30 minutes. Turn cakes out onto a wire rack to cool completely.

For filling and ganache:

1. Place chocolate in a large bowl. In a small saucepan, warm cream until it comes to a simmer. Remove from heat and immediately pour cream over chocolate. Stir until blended and glossy. Cool ganache to room temperature.
2. Place 1 cake layer on a serving platter, domed-side down. Spread prepared caramel over layer. Cut about 12 candies in half; press into caramel. Top with remaining cake, rounded side up. Spread cooled ganache over the top and sides of cake. Pile remaining candies in a mound in the center of the cake.

Christmas Morning Chocolate Swirl Buns

Start a family tradition and make a special breakfast treat to serve every Christmas morning. This recipe makes 4 giant buns. For classic smaller buns, roll the dough log, starting on the long end, and cut into 12 buns.

Makes 4 giant buns

Dough

- 1 cup whole milk
- 3 tablespoons unsalted butter, cut into 4 pieces, plus additional for greasing bowl
- 3½ cups all-purpose flour, divided, plus additional for rolling out
- ½ cup granulated sugar
- 1 large egg
- 1 package (2¼ teaspoons) instant yeast
- ½ teaspoon salt

Filling

- 4 tablespoons (½ stick) unsalted butter, at room temperature
- ⅓ cup granulated sugar
- 1 cup (6 ounces) finely chopped semisweet chocolate (or mini-chocolate chips)

Icing

- 1 cup powdered sugar
- 3 tablespoons unsweetened cocoa
- 3–4 tablespoons whole milk, as needed

TIP: If you prefer the classic cinnamon flavor, substitute cinnamon sugar for the chopped chocolate.

Christmas Morning Chocolate Swirl Buns

Recipe continued from previous page.

For dough and filling:

1. In a glass measuring cup, combine milk and chopped butter. Microwave until butter melts. In the large bowl of an electric mixer, combine warm butter mixture, 1 cup of the flour, sugar, egg, yeast and salt. Mix on low speed for 2 minutes, until well blended. Add remaining 2½ cups flour; mix just until blended. If dough is too sticky, add additional flour until dough holds together and pulls away from the sides of the bowl. Dump dough out onto a lightly floured surface; knead for 5 minutes, until dough is smooth and elastic.
2. Lightly grease a large bowl. Form dough into a ball; place in the greased bowl and turn to coat. Cover the bowl with plastic wrap and a kitchen towel. Place the bowl in a warm area and let the dough rise for 2 hours, until doubled.
3. Line a large baking sheet with parchment paper. Turn the dough out onto a lightly floured surface; punch down dough and let it sit 5 minutes. Using a floured rolling pin, roll out the dough to a 10-by-20-inch rectangle. Spread 4 tablespoons butter over the dough. Sprinkle with sugar, then chopped chocolate. Starting from the short side, roll up the rectangle to a fat roll. Slice the rolled log into 4 equal pieces. Transfer buns to the prepared baking sheet. Cover with plastic wrap; place in a warm area and let rise 30 minutes. (At this point, dough can be covered and refrigerated overnight. Let stand 30 minutes at room temperature before continuing recipe.)
4. Preheat oven to 350°F. Bake rolls 30 to 35 minutes, until golden. Cover rolls in the last 10 minutes of baking if they're overbrowning. Let buns cool 5 minutes in the pan; transfer to a wire rack to cool completely.

For icing:

1. In a small bowl, whisk icing ingredients to drizzling consistency. Drizzle over cooled buns.

Layered Pear Cranberry Crumb Pie

Two classic holiday pies combined in one sweet, crumble-topped dessert.

Serves 10

Cranberry layer

- 2 cups fresh or frozen cranberries
- ¼ cup orange juice
- 1 cup granulated sugar, divided, plus additional for topping
- ½ teaspoon salt, divided
- ¼ cup water

Pears

- 6 medium ripe pears, peeled and thinly sliced
- ½ teaspoon ground cinnamon
- 1 tablespoon cornstarch
- ¼ cup water
- 1 prepared pie crust

Streusel topping

- ½ cup (1 stick) unsalted butter, melted
- ⅓ cup light-brown sugar
- ⅓ cup granulated sugar
- 1¼ cups all-purpose flour
- Pinch of salt

For cranberry layer:

1. In a small saucepan over medium heat, bring cranberries, juice, ½ cup of the sugar and ¼ teaspoon of the salt to a boil. Cook 10 minutes, until berries are soft and mixture is jamlike, stirring often and pressing berries against the side of the pot. Remove from heat, stir in ¼ cup water and let cool slightly.

For pears:

1. In a large microwave-safe bowl, combine pears with remaining ½ cup sugar, cinnamon, remaining ¼ teaspoon salt, cornstarch and ¼ cup water. Toss until pears are coated. Microwave 10 minutes, until pears are very tender and liquid thickens, stirring every few minutes. Let cool slightly.
2. Preheat oven to 425°F; set oven rack to the lowest position. Spoon the cooled cranberry mixture into the pie crust. Spoon pears on top of the cranberries, mounding slightly in the center.

For streusel topping:

1. In a medium bowl, stir melted butter and both sugars until sugar is dissolved. Stir in flour and salt until mixture forms a thick mass. Using your hands, crumble topping evenly over pears.
2. Place pie on a baking sheet. Bake 50 minutes, until golden brown and fruit is bubbling. Rotate baking sheet once during baking time. Transfer to a wire rack to cool. Let the pie cool 2 hours before serving.

CHAPTER 12

Greg's mouth was soft and tender. She leaned into him, prepared to lose herself in his kiss, only he pulled back and stared into her eyes.

"I have to tell you something."

What? He wanted to have a conversation now? Wasn't that just like a man.

"I'm in love with you."

Ana Raquel felt her mouth drop open. She consciously closed it. "I'm sorry. What did you just say?"

He smiled and touched her cheek. "I'm in love with you. I have been for years."

No way! It wasn't possible. She'd just been thinking that and now he was saying it? Was someone playing a trick on her?

"I lost my heart to you when I was seven," he admitted. "The first time I saw you dressed up as Cinderella. The reason I acted the way I did onstage, overacting, talking over everyone's lines, I was afraid I was going to blurt out the truth."

His dark gaze locked with hers. "I only ran for student council president because you were and I thought it would be fun for us to hang out. I never thought I'd win. As for what happened after prom..."

He touched his mouth to hers. "You were my first time, too," he whispered.

She desperately wanted to believe him, but there were too many questions. "You always had a girlfriend."

He shrugged. "I was trying to get your attention."

"You didn't come after me when I left."

"We were kids and needed to grow up. And, honestly, after you left so quickly, I thought you didn't like me. But I kept track of you. Ask your sisters."

She didn't have to, she realized. Both Dellina and Fayrene had always teased her about Greg. Now she knew why.

Disbelief battled with a sense of certainty. There was only one reason she'd gotten so worked up whenever she thought about Greg. Only one reason she hadn't been able to stop thinking about him. It was because she'd had feelings, too.

"Back then, it was a crush. But knowing you now… I love you," he repeated. "I don't want you here just as my business partner. I want you as my everything partner. I know it's a lot to take in, but will you at least think about it?"

She tried to speak but couldn't, then decided the words could wait. She threw herself into his arms and hung on as if she would never let go.

"We can do it all," he was saying. "The restaurant and your street food. We can even try another cookbook."

She started to laugh, then realized she was crying. Happy tears, she thought. Because she'd found the man who could be her life partner. Who could understand her dreams because he shared them.

She drew back enough to see his face. "I love you, too. I think I have for a long time."

"You were mostly pissed at me."

She laughed. "A little. Sometimes. You can be really annoying."

"I'll try to change that."

"I'd rather you didn't. I like what we have together. And, yes, let's do it all. The restaurant and the street food. We'll use one to promote the other. We'll be a team."

He drew her against him and kissed her again. She got lost in the feel of him and how being near him made every part of her tingle.

On the table, the champagne went flat and the dinner cooled, but Ana Raquel didn't even notice. Greg's kisses were more delicious than food, more intoxicating than champagne.

They were in love, she thought with a sigh. Fool's Gold really was the land of happy endings.

Fin

Fool's Gold Characters

Where It All Began

CHASING PERFECT
FOOL'S GOLD 1

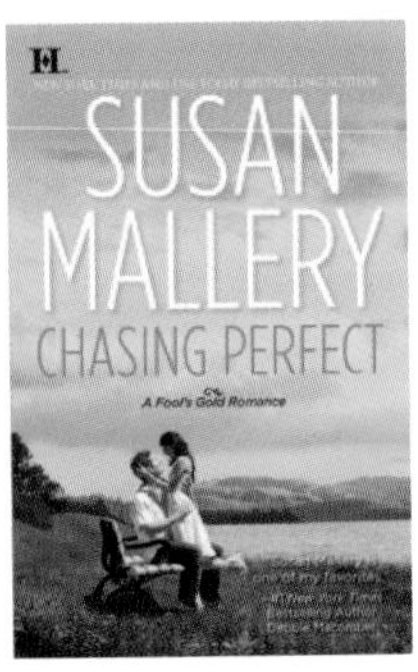

Charity Golden (maiden name Jones): Charity Jones is an accomplished City Planner who's not nearly as good at planning her own future. She's always chasing the perfect job, the perfect life. When the city of Fool's Gold comes calling, Charity is convinced that the small town is the perfect place for her to settle down... except for one pesky detail: she can't get through a single day without running into sexy athlete Josh Golden, a man who plays havoc with her peace of mind. Josh is all wrong for her. He dates movie stars and models, lives life in the fast lane. So why do his kisses feel so... perfect?

Josh Golden: Josh Golden is hiding something. He's not nearly as perfect as everyone in Fool's Gold thinks he is. A fatal accident has left the former Tour de France winner with scars that no one can see. No one, that is, except the town's newest resident, Charity Jones. From the moment they meet, she sees right through his "everything's fine" charade. The question is, will she expose him as the fraud he is? If he knew what was good for him, he would stay far away from her perceptive brown eyes. But Josh has always been attracted to danger, and sweet little Charity just may be the most dangerous woman he's ever met.

Fiona Golden: Charity and Josh's first baby, born on Groundhog Day 2011. Josh wanted to name her Philippa after Punxsutawney Phil from the movie *Groundhog Day*! Read about Fiona's birth and Charity and Josh's celebrity wedding on the News page at www.foolsgoldca.com.

Hunter Golden: Charity and Josh's second baby was born on March 18, 2013. Big sister Fiona is thrilled. (Hunter was named by a reader on Susan's Facebook page, www.facebook.com/susanmallery. Join the fun!)

Marsha Tilson: Mayor Marsha Tilson is the longest-serving mayor in the state of California. She first stepped into office when she was twenty-six, a young widow looking for a way to make a difference. Now she seems to know everything about everyone, but no one minds because Marsha is always respectful and helpful. How is it possible that this wonderful woman was estranged from her own daughter for so long?

ALMOST PERFECT
FOOL'S GOLD 2

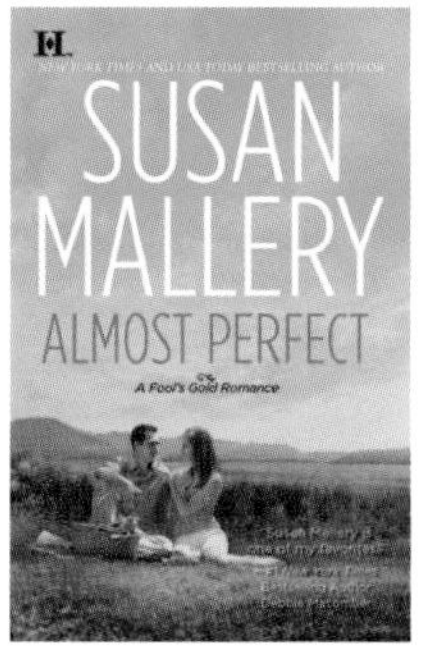

Liz Sutton: When bestselling mystery author Liz Sutton was a teenager, she fell in love with Ethan Hendrix, one of the hottest guys in town. And he loved her, even though her family was poor and not exactly respectable! At least, she thought he loved her, until she heard him deny their secret relationship to his friends. Wounded and pregnant, she ran away, with no intention of ever returning to her hometown. Until her phone rings years later, and a small voice on the other end of the line says, "Aunt Liz? We need you."

Liz can't resist the cry for help from her young nieces, even if it means seeing Ethan again and introducing him to the son she thought he never wanted to know.

Ethan Hendrix: Ethan Hendrix always regretted hurting Liz. He'd been young and weak and had tried to protect his family's strong ties in the community. Over the years, he has cheered Liz's success as a mystery author from afar, despite the fact that she keeps killing a character who looks suspiciously like him in every book. When Liz returns to Fool's Gold, he's thrilled to see her...until she introduces him to the son he hadn't known, the son she kept from him for ten years.

Abby Sutton: Liz's niece

Melissa Sutton: Liz's niece

Tyler Sutton: Liz and Ethan's son, who looks just like his dad, except that he has Liz's smile.

SISTER OF THE BRIDE
FOOL'S GOLD 2.5

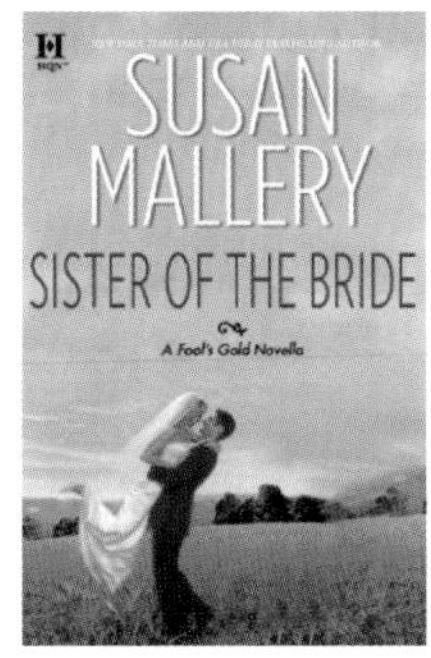

Katie Kent (maiden name McCormick): Sportswriter Katie McCormick dreads her sister's wedding. Who could blame her, when her sister is marrying Katie's ex? Mostly, Katie dreads the looks of pity she's sure to get when she shows up at the wedding without a date. So despite her better judgment, she finally agrees to let her mother set her up with super-nerd Howard "Jackson" Kent.

Howard (Jackson) Kent: Somewhere between graduating MIT and becoming a multimillionaire, software developer Jackson Kent left his nerd days far behind. He has no trouble getting his own dates and agrees to escort Katie during the wedding weekend only as a favor to his mother. But when he lays eyes on Katie for the first time since they were kids, he has a feeling he'll owe his mother a big thank-you instead of the other way around.

Alex Lumpkin: Can Alex help it that he fell in love with his girlfriend's sister? What was he supposed to do, NOT ask the woman he loved to marry him?

Courtney McCormick: Katie's somewhat self-involved younger sister, who isn't quite sure why Katie minds that she's marrying Katie's ex.

Janis McCormick: Katie's mom loves her daughters equally, so while she's happy Courtney found love, she wishes the girl hadn't fallen for Katie's boyfriend. No wonder she felt the need to get a little tipsy at the rehearsal dinner!

Mike McCormick: Life is good for Mike McCormick. He gets to play proud papa to walk his youngest down the aisle...and his older daughter, Katie, seems to have found a match, too. Now all Mike needs to make his happiness complete is a little nooky in the elevator with his sexy wife.

Aunt Tully: Katie's aunt, who has a bad habit of flirting with every man she meets—and sleeping with far too many of them!

Tina Kent: Tina doesn't hesitate to play the guilt card with her handsome son Jackson, if that's what it will take to get him to go on a date with Katie, her best friend's daughter. The two women have tried for years to get their kids together!

FINDING PERFECT
FOOL'S GOLD 3

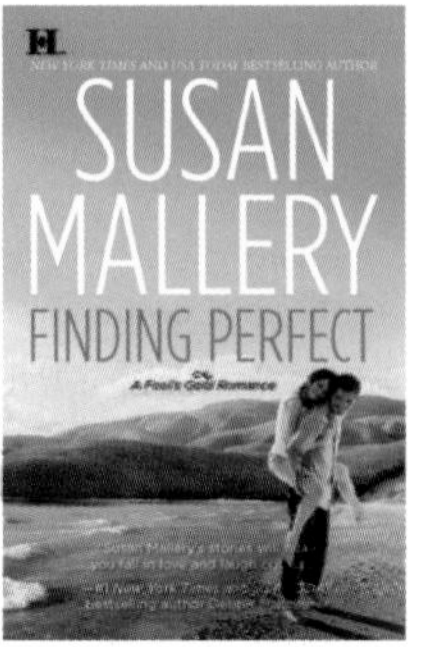

Pia Moreno (maiden name O'Brian): As the Fool's Gold event planner, Pia is a pro at multitasking, but this is taking things a little too far. Her best friend has left her with not one, not two, but three frozen embryos. Pia wants to honor her friend's final wish but is overwhelmed at the thought of being a single mother to triplets. While she's pregnant is no time to meet a man who makes her stomach do flips.

Raoul Moreno: Former professional quarterback Raoul Moreno grew up in the inner city and has moved to Fool's Gold to open a camp to give other city kids a taste of nature. Stung by love in the past, Raoul has no interest in settling down, now or ever. But how can he resist a woman like Pia, who's so honorable that she's willing to make the ultimate sacrifice for the sake of her late best friend? Loyalty like that doesn't come along every day...especially not wrapped in a package as sexy as Pia! Readers first met Raoul as a teenager in Susan Mallery's *Sweet Spot*.

Adelina and Rosabel Moreno: Pia and Raoul's twins, carried by Pia, but the biological children of Crystal, Pia's late best friend.

Peter Moreno: After his parents were killed in a terrible car accident, ten-year-old

Peter was alone in the world until he was adopted by Raoul and Pia.

Bun-in-the-Oven Moreno: Pia's pregnant again. The whole family is thrilled! Read *Christmas on 4th Street* to meet the newest Moreno.

Crystal Danes: When Crystal dies, she leaves her best friend Pia with a most unusual inheritance—both an unbelievable gift and an incredible burden—three fertilized embryos. Will Pia give life to her best friend's babies?

The Hendrix Triplets

ONLY MINE
FOOL'S GOLD 4

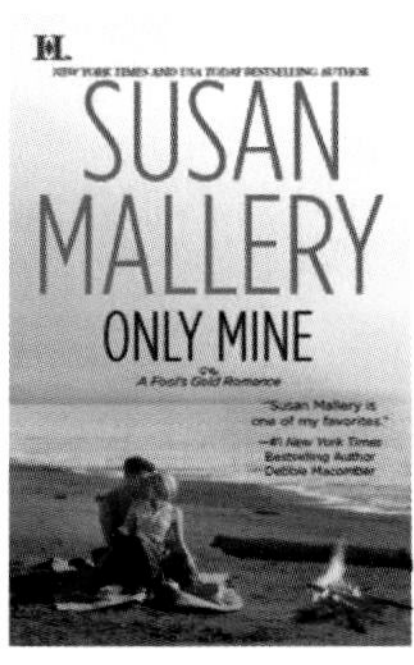

Dakota Andersson (maiden name Hendrix): Dakota should be happy. She has a job she loves in a hometown she adores. But Dakota has a secret that's breaking her heart, a secret buried so deep that even her identical triplet sisters don't know what's causing the pain in her eyes. If screening contestants for a reality dating show doesn't shake her out of the blues, maybe the arrival of stern and sexy Finn Andersson will.

Finn Andersson: Alaskan pilot Finn Andersson has weathered a lot of storms, including raising his brothers after the death of their parents. Freedom beckons with his brothers' long-anticipated college graduation—until the twins drop out to pursue fame on a silly TV show. Finn will do anything to get his brothers back in school where they belong...including facing off against the beautiful blonde with the sad eyes. Dakota insists he should let his brothers make their own decisions, even if they're wrong. Clearly the woman doesn't know the meaning of the word *family*.

Hannah Hendrix: Dakota and Finn's adopted daughter.

Jordan Taylor Andersson: Dakota and Finn's son, born in February 2012. Jordan Taylor's first word was *Hannah*, because he loves his big sister so much. Jordan Taylor was named by a reader on Susan's Facebook page, www.facebook.com/susanmallery.

Denise Hendrix: Widowed for ten years, Denise is beginning to feel restless. She loves her three sons and triplet daughters, and she loves her grandkids and hopes more will follow...but is that it for her? Or could there be a life still waiting for her, with a man who makes her heart beat faster? Denise finds love in a secondary romance in *Only His*.

Sasha Andersson: One of Finn's brothers. Sasha and his brother Stephen are twins, but are different in many ways. Sasha got his first taste of fame in the reality show *True Love or Fool's Gold*. Now he lives in L.A., where he's working as an actor. He plays a rookie cop on a prime-time drama.

Stephen Andersson: One of Finn's brothers. Stephen and his brother Sasha were both on the reality dating show *True Love* *or Fool's Gold.* While Sasha gained fame from the show, Stephen got something even better—true love with his girlfriend Aurelia, an older woman. Stephen falls in love in a secondary romance in *Only Mine.*

ONLY YOURS
FOOL'S GOLD 5

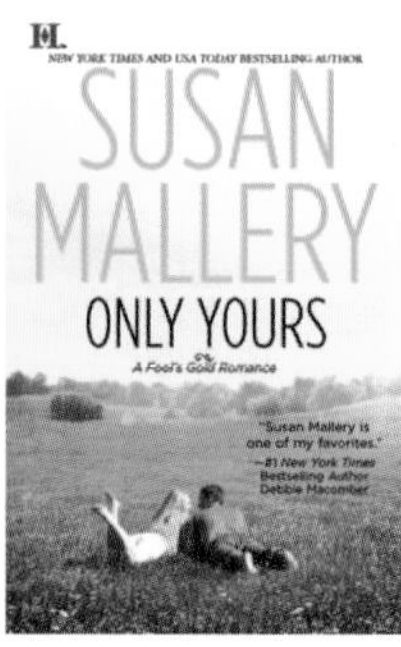

Montana Bradley (maiden name Hendrix): After years of moving from one job to the next, Montana has finally found the perfect career for her—training therapy dogs. Now she's ready for life's next step—marriage and kids. But the last man she would be intrigued by is dangerously sexy Dr. Simon Bradley. He may be brilliant, but Montana wants nothing to do with a man who can't find humor in the antics of a clumsy mutt. Except...Simon is unbelievably gentle with his pediatric patients, and his nimble fingers, trained for surgery, can do amazing things to her body. Maybe, just maybe, a bad first impression can turn into a lifetime of romance.

Simon Bradley: Pediatric burn specialist Simon Bradley has traveled the world saving lives, but he's never been anywhere like Fool's Gold. The friendly town pulls out all the stops to convince him to stick around, including sending alluring Montana Hendrix to be his personal tour guide. Simon learned long ago that he could find safety in the number one, but Montana's sweet kisses and caring nature might convince the vagabond surgeon that making a home is worth risking the heart.

Skye Bradley: Simon and Montana's baby daughter. Skye's mouth is a perfect little rosebud. (Skye was named by a reader on Susan's Facebook page, www.facebook.com/susanmallery. Join the fun!)

Kalinda Riley: Kalinda is a pediatric patient of Simon's. Kalinda was burned in a terrible accident in her family's backyard. She and her mother have been virtually adopted by the people of Fool's Gold, and Kalinda is getting better every day. She felt happier after Reese Hendrix promised to marry her someday if she couldn't find a husband.

ONLY HIS
FOOL'S GOLD 6

Nevada Janack (maiden name Hendrix): With both of her triplet sisters happily engaged and no romantic prospects on the horizon for her, engineer Nevada puts all her attention on her career. She's determined to prove herself away from the family business. Unfortunately for her, she discovers that her new boss is none other than the first man who ever saw her naked...and the first man who broke her heart. Could she survive losing Tucker a second time around?

Tucker Janack: In Fool's Gold to build a fabulous casino resort, Tucker Janack will never again allow love to consume him. Instead, he intends to focus on expanding his multimillion-dollar construction empire. That means hiring the best woman for the job, even if she inspires fantasies that have nothing to do with work.

Hendrix Janack: Hendrix was born on March 19, 2013, one week after his due date. Nevada tried all sorts of things to try to get labor started, but Hendrix had a schedule of his own. Check out the News page at www.foolsgoldca.com to read about Hendrix's birth and other between-the-books updates! (Hendrix was named by a reader on Susan's Facebook page, www.facebook.com/susanmallery.)

Caterina Stoicasescu: Tucker's ex-girlfriend Caterina is a world-famous sculptress known for pushing art in sometimes shocking directions. The women of Fool's Gold are somewhat aghast about the "gift" that Caterina is determined to bestow upon the town.

Jo Trellis: Ever since Jo arrived in Fool's Gold in 2006, rumors have swirled about her. Is she a mafia princess in witness protection? Is she on the run from an abusive husband? No one knows, and Jo's not telling. Jo finds love in a secondary romance in *Only His*.

Will Falk: Will Falk is a man of few words, but there's a lot of strength in his silence. He's Tucker's right-hand man, in charge of multimillion-dollar construction projects. Will admires strong women, particularly Jo, the owner of Jo's Bar. But when he discovers the truth about Jo's past, will he still want her? Will falls in love in a secondary romance in *Only His*.

Max Thurman: Max is a man of mystery when he first arrives in Fool's Gold and opens K9Rx Therapy Dog Kennels. With steel-gray hair and piercing blue eyes, Max is proof that some men grow better with age. The Hendrix kids wonder—could this be the same Max whose name has been tattooed on their mom's hip all these years? Max falls in love with Denise Hendrix in a secondary romance in *Only His*.

ONLY US
FOOL'S GOLD 6.5

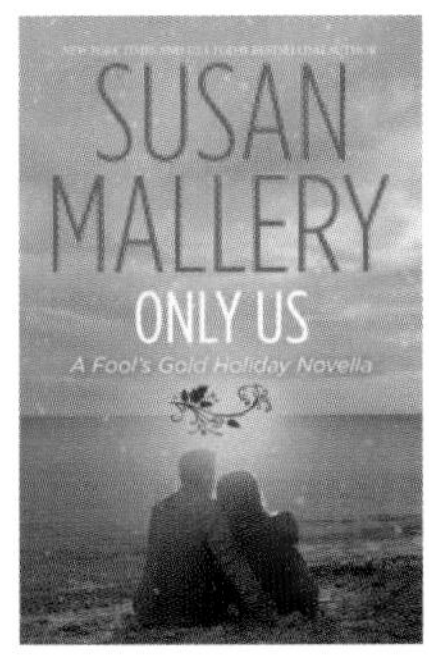

Carina (Rina) McKenzie (maiden name Fiore): Pet groomer Rina has a problem: she's in love with her boss. Cameron is kind, loves animals and children, and he's sexy, too. Unfortunately, he sees Rina as nothing more than an employee and part-time nanny to his precocious daughter. If Rina confesses her feelings, she could lose them both forever...but if she doesn't, she might be doomed to spend another Christmas alone. Rina was named by a fan at www.facebook.com/susanmallery, so she was given the fan's last name.

Cameron McKenzie: Cameron McKenzie doesn't need romance. His veterinary practice in Fool's Gold fulfills him at work, and his daughter keeps him from getting lonely at home. His life is very...okay. Why, then, has he suddenly begun to notice that Rina's eyes are as blue as the December sky? And why does he keep thinking of new spots to hang mistletoe? Cameron falls in love in *Only Us*, a novella. (Cameron was created by Susan's Facebook friends. Join the fun at www.facebook.com/susanmallery!)

Kaitlyn Leigh McKenzie: Cameron's adorable daughter. Rina used her pet-grooming experience to do Kaitlyn's hair before school every day, and they grew as close as mother and daughter.

The Year of the Cowboy

ALMOST SUMMER
FOOL'S GOLD 6.75

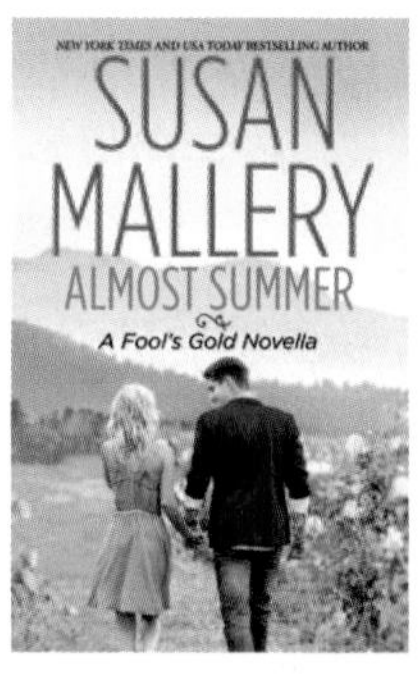

Paige Woodbury (maiden name McLean): Although she loves Fool's Gold, yoga instructor Paige McLean longs to see the world. Until now, fear has kept her from hopping on the next plane overseas. When "the world" lands on her doorstep in the form of a sexy British doctor in need of some TLC—a viscount, no less—Paige thinks that maybe, just maybe, she simply didn't want to fly alone. Paige was named by a fan at www.facebook.com/susanmallery, so she was given the fan's last name.

Alistair Woodbury: Since the tragic loss of his wife, surgeon Alistair Woodbury hasn't lingered long in any one place. When circumstances force him to stay in Paige's house, her bright smile and caring nature make the good doctor wonder whether solitude is the prescription for what ails him, after all.

SUMMER DAYS
FOOL'S GOLD 7

Heidi Stryker (maiden name Simpson):

After a vagabond childhood, goatherd Heidi is living the life of her dreams. She finally has a home to call her own. At least she thought she did, until she lands in court, facing off against sexy, angry Rafe Stryker, who is convinced that the Castle Ranch belongs to his family, not hers.

Rafe Stryker: To protect his family's interests, developer Rafe Stryker will become the one thing he swore he would never be again—a cowboy. He'll work the land of the Castle Ranch, land his mother rightfully owns, until the judge decides their fate. What he won't allow himself to do is fall for Heidi's fresh face and guileless green eyes...and he refuses to be tempted by her milkmaid-voluptuous body.

Clara Stryker: Heidi and Rafe welcomed little Clara into the world on July 7, 2013, while the rest of Fool's Gold celebrated the Fourth of July Festival. Read about her arrival in *Two of a Kind*. (Clara was named by a reader on Susan's Facebook page, www.facebook.com/susanmallery.)

Glen Simpson: Heidi's grandfather Glen is a bit of a rebel...which is catnip to women of a certain age. Glen is a very popular new arrival in Fool's Gold, but one special woman wins his heart. Glen falls in love in a secondary romance in *Summer Days.*

May Simpson (formerly Stryker): May is a loving mom to her three grown sons, Rafe, Shane and Clay. However, her relationship with daughter Evie has been strained. May knows she should love her children equally, but when she looks at Evie, she sees the one-night stand she had while grieving her beloved husband. May falls in love in a secondary romance in *Summer Days.*

SUMMER NIGHTS
FOOL'S GOLD 8

Annabelle Weiss: Librarian Annabelle Weiss longs for the kind of happy ending she reads about in books, but at twenty-seven, she's starting to wonder whether she'll ever meet The One. Her best friend Heidi recently got engaged—maybe there's hope for her yet! Except...Shane Stryker, the only man who's caught her eye in years, thinks that she's too dangerous to date. Annabelle was named by a fan at www.facebook.com/susanmallery, so she was given the fan's last name. (Annabelle is Susan's gift to librarians who were sick of the nerd-in-a-cardigan stereotype.)

Shane Stryker: Shane Stryker can tame any wild horse, but he doesn't have the same luck with women. Love has kicked him in the gut. He wants no part of it, wants no part of passion. Which is why he's determined to stay far, far away from the petite redhead with the killer body and a mouth made for kissing. Annabelle is far sexier than a librarian ought to be!

Wyatt Stryker: Baby Wyatt was a surprise to Annabelle and Shane—the happiest surprise of their lives. Born on April 18, 2013, Wyatt already shows signs of being a future cowboy like his daddy *and* a bookworm like his mommy. (Wyatt was named by Susan's Facebook friends.)

ALL SUMMER LONG
FOOL'S GOLD 9

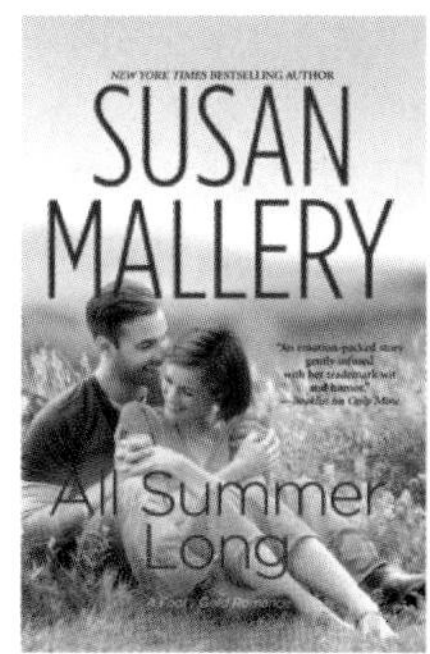

Charlie Dixon: As a firefighter, Charlie Dixon has risked her life many times without a moment's hesitation. But to risk her heart? That scares her to death. A trauma from her past is keeping her from moving forward with her life. When Clay Stryker comes to her for help to make the squad, she wants to refuse...but Clay is being judged solely on his looks, and Charlie knows how much that hurts. Maybe Clay can help her in return. For some reason, this dangerously sexy guy is the only man who makes her feel safe.

Clay Stryker: As an underwear model and Hollywood butt double, Clay Stryker amassed a fortune, so it shouldn't bother him that even in Fool's Gold, everyone judges him for his looks. Everyone, that is, except strong and stubborn Charlie Dixon, the most genuine person he's ever met. Now, if only he could convince her that inner beauty is what he's been looking for all along.

Dominique Guerin: Dominique Guerin may have been a world-class prima ballerina, but she wouldn't have won any awards for being a mother, as far as her daughter Charlie was concerned. Dominique always cared more about her audience than her own child, and at a critical moment in Charlie's life, her mother failed to stand up for her wounded daughter. Can Charlie ever forgive her?

A FOOL'S GOLD CHRISTMAS
FOOL'S GOLD 9.5

Evangeline (Evie) Jefferson (maiden name Stryker): The holiday spirit in Fool's Gold is hard to resist, even for dancer Evie Stryker, who learned at an early age to protect her heart by keeping her distance. She was the family afterthought, and they made sure she knew it. She finds an ally in handsome Dante Jefferson, a fellow outsider in this too-perfect-to-be-real world. But is Dante—her brother's best friend—really on her side? Or are his mistletoe kisses part of the conspiracy to convince her that Christmas miracles really do come true?

Dante Jefferson: During his delinquent youth, Dante Jefferson learned that love can be deadly, and he's been a lone wolf ever since. But then his business partner fell in love and moved to a small town in the mountains of California, and Dante finds himself in his own personal version of hell, with clog-dancing children thumping in the studio above his office. Unfortunately, the sexy dance instructor is none other than Evie, his business partner's sister…firmly off-limits, no matter how tempting she may be.

The Year of the Bodyguard

HALFWAY THERE
FOOL'S GOLD 9.75

Fayrene Hopkins: After her parents died when she was young, Fayrene felt safe only when she followed a very specific life plan. And the plan does not include love for another three years! Even if a certain sexy young man has been tempting her with late-night kisses.

Ryan Patterson: Wind engineer Ryan Patterson was happy to come to Fool's Gold on a temporary assignment, but once he discovers the town's most precious natural resource—Fayrene—he may not be able to make himself leave.

JUST ONE KISS
FOOL'S GOLD 10

Patience McGraw: Patience's first love disappeared overnight, without a trace, so she's thrilled when Justice reappears in Fool's Gold just as suddenly. But how can she ever trust that the handsome bodyguard won't leave her again? This time, her young daughter's heart could be broken, too.

Justice Garrett: Justice has never forgotten sweet, sassy Patience, the girl who stole his heart during his year in Fool's Gold, where witness protection hid him from his dangerous father. When Justice returns to town to open an elite defense academy, he can't resist seeing her again, even though he knows the last thing he should do, with the darkness inside him, is touch her.

Lillie McGraw: Patience's nine-year-old daughter, who loves to dance but isn't very good at it. (Shh! Don't tell her!)

Ava: Patience's mother, who struggles with the symptoms of MS but tries hard not to let them get her down. Ava has a secret she's been keeping from Patience. When her daughter learns the truth, will she forgive Ava for her deception?

TWO OF A KIND
FOOL'S GOLD 11

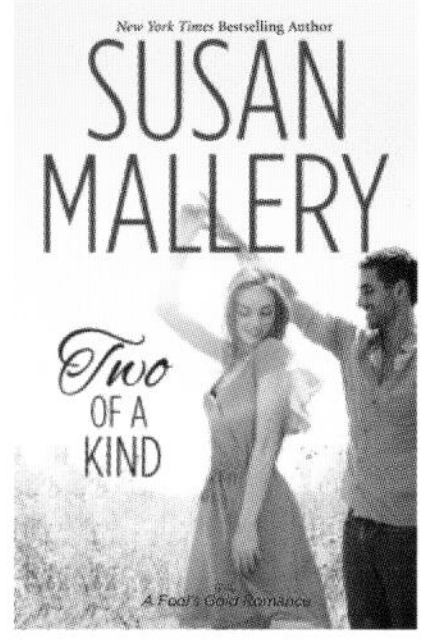

Felicia Swift: Felicia just might be the smartest person in the world, but after being raised on a university campus, she feels socially awkward and wants nothing more than to be normal, to fit in. Maybe Gideon, the man she seduced into taking her virginity, can teach her how people behave when they're in love.

Gideon Boylan: Gideon Boylan spent two years in a Taliban prison, where he learned that loving someone makes you vulnerable. He won't allow himself to go there. So when smart, sexy Felicia asks him to help learn how to be in a real relationship, he's confident he can play boyfriend for a time without risking his heart.

Carter Gates: Ever since his mom died, Carter's heart has ached with loneliness, but he hides his tears from the world. He's brave, strong—traits he got from the father he's never met? Only one way to find out: track down his dad!

THREE LITTLE WORDS
FOOL'S GOLD 12

Isabel Beebe: When Isabel agreed to run her parents' bridal boutique, she didn't know hometown hero Ford Hendrix would also be back in Fool's Gold. Now she's ducking around corners to avoid the handsome ex-SEAL, her unrequited first love—the man she wrote to for years, confessing her teenage dreams. He never replied, not once, and now that she's all grown up, she's embarrassed about the secrets he knows. Isabel was named by a fan at www.facebook.com/susanmallery, so she was given the fan's last name.

Ford Hendrix: After years as a Navy SEAL, Ford is coming home to Fool's Gold to open an elite defense academy with some former military buddies. He's not sure how he feels about living so close to his family again. He loves them, but will they understand that he is no longer the same person he once was? He has seen things, done things that changed him inside.

Consuelo Ly: Feisty Consuelo can take down a trained fighter twice her size, but facing a small-town math teacher with a heart of gold intimidates the hell out of her. If Kent knew the truth about her, he'd stop looking at her with love in his eyes, she's sure of it. Consuelo finds love in a secondary romance in *Three Little Words*.

Kent Hendrix: Kent, the second of the Hendrix boys, hasn't been lucky in love. His wife abandoned him and their son, Reese, and for a long time Kent has wanted nothing more than to have his wife back. But is she the right woman for him? His mom, Denise, certainly doesn't think so! Kent falls in love in a secondary romance in *Three Little Words*.

Maeve Turner: Isabel's sister Maeve made a mistake many years ago, but her mistake wasn't in jilting Ford—it was in getting engaged to him in the first place. Now happily married to Leonard and popping out babies, Maeve might be the only person in Fool's Gold who isn't exactly excited that Ford's coming home.

Leonard Turner: Leonard's worst fear has come true. His wife's ex-fiancé and his former best friend, Ford Hendrix, is coming home. Has Ford ever forgiven them for breaking his heart?

Reese Hendrix: Reese, Kent Hendrix's son, is a great kid. It's too bad that his mom virtually abandoned him. Her loss. Reese has a terrific heart and Fool's Gold is lucky to have him.

SUSAN MALLERY'S FOOL'S GOLD COOKBOOK
SHORT STORY

Ana Raquel Hopkins: Ana Raquel's parents died when she was young, and she and her sisters were split up and sent away from Fool's Gold. Now, finally, she's back and ready to open the first street food trailer the town has ever seen. She's thrilled to be back in her beloved hometown, but not nearly as thrilled when Mayor Marsha asks her to work with her childhood nemesis to put together a cookbook with the town's favorite recipes.

Greg Clary: Restaurateur Greg Clary is happy when Mayor Marsha asks him to help Ana Raquel write the Fool's Gold cookbook. No one says no to Mayor Marsha, which means Ana Raquel will have to stop running away from him the way she has done since their senior prom six years ago. And maybe Greg will finally get the chance to tell Ana Raquel how he feels.

CHRISTMAS ON 4TH STREET
FOOL'S GOLD 12.5

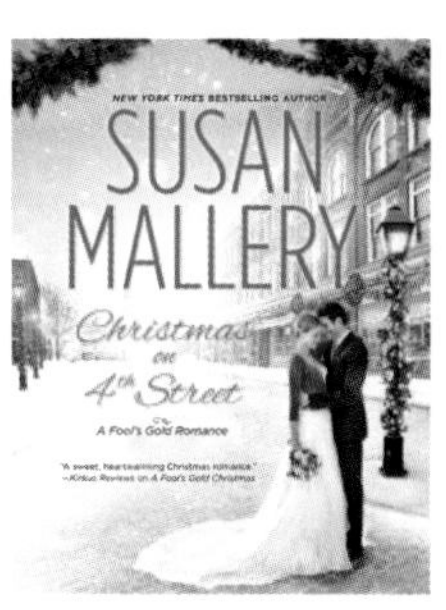

Noelle Perkins: Noelle has good reasons for wanting to grab life with both hands. On impulse one day, she spun around, put a pin in the map and moved to Fool's Gold to open the Christmas store she'd always dreamed of. Next step, find love. Except...Gabriel, the only man to tempt her, thinks love is too dangerous. Why can't he see that the real risk is never loving at all?

Gabriel Boylan: Gabriel Boylan is Gideon's fair-haired twin brother, the one who played by all the rules, became a surgeon on the Army's dime. Working with wounded soldiers convinced him that death is too near for him to ever risk falling in love. But Noelle's Christmas cheer—and her beauty—just might be enough to heal his warrior heart.

Visit the Freebies page at SusanMallery.com for a printable Who's Who in Fool's Gold that includes other recurring characters!

Acknowledgments

While I desperately want to take credit for a cookbook this beautiful and fun, there is simply no way I could have done it by myself. The list of notables who helped is significant and I want to thank each of them.

Tara, Annelise and Jenel—you are my team, my peeps, my friends. You each bring a unique perspective to what I do and my world would be much smaller without you.

Deb and the Harlequin team—this beautiful book is the result of hours of work and attention, and I appreciate all that was done.

Susie—you took a tattered list of recipes and comments like "In Fool's Gold, as in my regular life, guacamole is a major food group" and turned it into delicious magic.

Debbie Macomber—friend, mentor and brilliant author. In 2008 Debbie said to me: "Your family books are great. Now write about a town." Advice for which I will always be grateful.

To my cheerleaders, past and present. I love what you do, I am forever appreciative and Fool's Gold is a far better place because you care.

Last but not least, to my readers. You are loyal, supportive and quite discerning in your taste in books! ☺ Seriously, you lift me up when I'm struggling, you inspire me with your personal stories and you allow me to do what I most love. There aren't enough words to thank you. I hope when you make these recipes, you'll think of me and know that I am sending love back.

Happy reading, happy cooking and, most important of all, happy eating, my friends.

About the Author

With more than 25 million books sold worldwide, *New York Times* bestselling author Susan Mallery is known for creating characters who feel as real as the folks next door, and for putting them into emotional, often funny situations readers recognize from their own lives. Susan's books have made Booklist's Top 10 Romances list in four out of five consecutive years. *RT Book Reviews* says, "When it comes to heartfelt contemporary romance, Mallery is in a class by herself." With her popular, ongoing Fool's Gold series, Susan has reached new heights on the bestsellers lists and has won the hearts of countless new fans.

Susan grew up in southern California, moved so many times that her friends stopped writing her address in pen, and now has settled in Seattle with her husband and the most delightfully spoiled little dog who ever lived. Visit Susan online at www.SusanMallery.com.

Conversion Charts

Volume

U.S. Volume Unit	Metric Equivalent
1 teaspoon	5 milliliters
1 tablespoon or ½ fluid ounce	15 milliliters
1 fluid ounce or ⅛ cup	30 milliliters
¼ cup or 2 fluid ounces	60 milliliters
⅓ cup	80 milliliters
½ cup or 4 fluid ounces	120 milliliters
⅔ cup	160 milliliters
¾ cup or 6 fluid ounces	180 milliliters
1 cup or 8 fluid ounces or ½ pint	240 milliliters
1½ cups or 12 fluid ounces	350 milliliters
2 cups or 1 pint or 16 fluid ounces	475 milliliters
3 cups or 1½ pints	700 milliliters
4 cups or 2 pints or 1 quart	950 milliliters
4 quarts or 1 gallon	3.8 liters

Temperature

Fahrenheit	Celsius
212°	100°
250°	120°
275°	140°
300°	150°
325°	160°
350°	180°
375°	190°
400°	200°
425°	220°
450°	230°
475°	240°
500°	260°

Weight

U.S. Weight Unit		Metric Equivalent
1 ounce		28 grams
4 ounces	¼ pound	113 grams
	⅓ pound	150 grams
8 ounces	½ pound	230 grams
	⅔ pound	300 grams
12 ounces	¾ pound	340 grams
16 ounces	1 pound	450 grams
	2 pounds	900 grams
	2.2 pounds	1 kilogram

Index

E

F

Q

R

S

T

W

Z